CONTENTS

FIGURE

TABLE

PREFACE

In June 1995, the leaders of the major industrial countries, meeting in Halifax, made several proposals aimed at applying the lessons learned during the Mexican crisis of 1994–95. A year later, at their meeting in Lyons, they were able to note that significant progress had been made in implementing their proposals. This Essay contains four short papers reflecting on the proposals made at the Halifax Summit and the steps taken thereafter. It begins with an Introduction by Lawrence H. Summers, Deputy Secretary of the U.S. Treasury, and includes contributions by William R. Cline, Barry Eichengreen and Richard Portes, Arminio Fraga, and Morris Goldstein. A few words about the authors follow:

Lawrence H. Summers has served as Deputy Secretary of the U.S. Treasury since August 1995 and for two years before that, as Undersecretary of the Treasury for International Affairs. From 1991 to 1993, he was Vice President of Development Economics and Chief Economist at the World Bank. He was a domestic policy economist on the President's Council of Economic Advisors in 1982–83, taught at the Massachusetts Institute of Technology from 1979 to 1982, and joined the Harvard University faculty in 1983. He has written extensively on economic analysis and policy.

William R. Cline is Deputy Managing Director and Chief Economist at the Institute of International Finance. His publications on the subject of international debt include, most recently, *International Debt Reexamined* (1995).

Barry Eichengreen is John L. Simpson Professor of Economics and Professor of Political Science at the University of California, Berkeley. Professor Eichengreen has written extensively on the history and prospects of the international monetary system. He is the coauthor, with Richard Portes, of *Crisis? What Crisis? Orderly Workouts for Sovereign Debtors* (1995). This is his fifth contribution to the publications of the International Finance Section.

Richard Portes is Director of the Centre for Economic Policy Research, Professor of Economics at the London School of Business, and Directeur d'Études, École des Hautes Études en Sciences Sociales (at DELTA), Paris. He is the coauthor, with Barry Eichengreen, of *Crisis?*

What Crisis? Orderly Workouts for Sovereign Debtors (1995) and a contributing author to the International Finance Section's *Europe After 1992: Three Essays* (1991).

Arminio Fraga is Managing Director of Soros Fund Management and Adjunct Professor at the School of International and Public Affairs at Columbia University. He served as Director of International Affairs at the Central Bank of Brazil from 1991 to 1992. His publications include an Essay with the International Finance Section, *German Reparations and Brazilian Debt: A Comparative Study* (1986).

Morris Goldstein is Dennis Weatherstone Senior Fellow at the Institute for International Economics and a former Deputy Director of Research at the International Monetary Fund. He is the coeditor of *Private Capital Flows to Emerging Markets After the Mexican Crisis* (Calvo, Goldstein, and Hochreiter, 1996), the author of *The Exchange Rate System and the IMF: A Modest Agenda* (1995), and the author of a Special Paper with the International Finance Section, *Have Flexible Exchange Rates Handicapped Macroeconomic Policy?* (1980).

This Essay concludes by reproducing the executive summary of the Group of Ten's report on "The Resolution of Sovereign Liquidity Crises," prepared in response to a request made at the Halifax Summit and endorsed subsequently at Lyons.

Peter B. Kenen

INTRODUCTION

Lawrence H. Summers

At the Halifax Summit, in June 1995, the leaders of the G–7 countries proposed several steps to strengthen the international financial system and to apply the lessons taught by the Mexican crisis of 1994–95. Most of those steps have now been taken. They represent a cohesive response to the most challenging problem facing the international financial system—the risk that a country experiencing large capital inflows will have suddenly to cope with large outflows when market participants revise their views about the country's prospects.

Many developing countries are now involved actively in international financial markets and benefit greatly from them. But they run two risks:

• Markets collect and assess information, and they do it rather well. That is why we rely on them to allocate savings, domestically and internationally. But market participants can change their views abruptly, forcing borrowers to change their policies abruptly. That is what happened to Mexico.

• With integrated financial markets, crises are contagious. When one country runs into trouble, market participants will ask whether others are vulnerable too, and even those with sound policies and prospects may have to fend off speculative pressures. That is what happened to several countries during the Mexican crisis.

It is therefore vital for countries involved in global financial markets to manage their economies prudently and to respond promptly to changes in economic and financial conditions both at home and abroad. There is no substitute for crisis prevention.

Many economists have become enamored of models that produce multiple equilibria and can therefore generate self-fulfilling crises; a spontaneous change in expectations about future conditions or policies induces a speculative attack that is then validated—not quelled—by policy changes. But expectations rarely change spontaneously, although they may change suddenly, and a country's susceptibility to crises depends mainly on the quality of its policy fundamentals. Crises typically occur when conditions or policies change—or when markets lose confidence in a government's willingness or ability to correct policy errors and adjust to new economic conditions. Unfortunately, governments sometimes squander the confidence that markets have vested in them. They pursue inconsistent exchange-rate and monetary policies, as Mexico did, or hope that bad news will be followed by good news, sparing them the need to alter their policies.

Some of the steps proposed by the Halifax Summit were aimed at encouraging governments and markets to pay closer attention to economic conditions in order to prevent crises from erupting:

- The International Monetary Fund (IMF) was urged to intensify its surveillance of national policies, give "sharper policy advice to all governments," and deliver "franker messages" to those that appear to be avoiding necessary policy changes. In the past, the IMF has relied mainly on annual consultations with its members, as mandated by its Articles of Agreement. These annual reviews were appropriate to a world in which balance-of-payments problems were caused mainly by slow-moving changes in current-account balances. They need now to be supplemented by the continuous monitoring of capital-account developments, with attention given to the composition of capital flows, potential liquidity problems, and the possible reaction of capital markets to political shocks.

- The IMF was also urged to establish benchmarks for the timely publication of economic and financial statistics and to develop methods for identifying publicly countries that comply with those standards. It has responded by adopting a two-tiered approach. It has developed a "general" standard for the publication of economic and financial statistics, toward which it will work with all governments, and a special data dissemination standard (SDDS) aimed at countries involved in international capital markets and those that aspire to participate in them. The IMF will not publish the data provided under the SDDS or assess their quality, but it will identify on the Internet those countries that meet the new standard, and it will supply information about the data to help users acquire and interpret them.

The Halifax Summit also proposed steps to assist the IMF and major national governments to respond effectively when crisis prevention fails and crises actually occur:

- The Summit urged the IMF to develop a procedure to provide faster access to IMF credit and larger up-front disbursements in crisis situations. It emphasized the need, however, for strong conditionality even in these special situations. The Fund responded by adopting an emergency-financing mechanism (EFM), designed to facilitate close consultation between the Fund's management and its executive board, which represents its member governments, during the Fund's negotiations with a country seeking financial support in a crisis situation.

• The Summit called on the Group of Ten (G–10) countries and other countries not previously involved to double the credit facilities available to the IMF under the General Arrangements to Borrow (GAB). The G–10 countries responded by entering into discussions among themselves and with other potential participants, and these have now led to an agreement under which the existing GAB will remain in place but will be surrounded by a new borrowing arrangement, in which the G–10 countries will be joined by several others. The arrangement will double the amount of credit available to the IMF under terms and conditions similar to those governing use of the GAB, and it will be the "first and principal" recourse for the IMF. A detailed agreement should be ready for adoption in time for the 1996 Annual Meeting of the IMF.

• Finally, the Halifax Summit asked that the finance ministers and central-bank governors of the G–10 countries review other procedures that might contribute to the orderly resolution of future financial crises. The G–10 countries responded by establishing a working party, under the chairmanship of Jean Jacques Ray of the National Bank of Belgium, which submitted its report to the ministers and governors in May 1996.

The working party examined a number of approaches to the resolution of financial crises, surveyed the views of market participants in several countries, and studied the legal issues involved in the resolution of financial crises. It paid close attention to the problems posed by the most challenging innovation of the last few years—the great growth of international capital movements reflecting transactions in securitized debt.

Arrangements for orderly debt workouts already exist for debts to sovereign lenders (the Paris Club) and debts to commercial banks (the London Club). These have functioned reasonably well, because the number of principal actors has been relatively small, so free-rider problems have been manageable. But thousands of mutual funds and bond holders have now replaced commercial banks as the main providers of private capital to developing countries, greatly complicating the management of future debt workouts, not only because the number of investors is so large, but also because those investors, unlike creditor governments and commercial banks, are unlikely to have an abiding interest in the economic future of a debtor country.

One approach to the problems considered by the working party, an international bankruptcy procedure, was discussed extensively during the debt crisis of the 1980s and has recently been advocated by Jeffrey Sachs. In his Graham Lecture at Princeton University, Sachs drew an extended analogy between the needs of a sovereign debtor and the forms of protection afforded by domestic bankruptcy laws. He emphasized the need to prevent a "grab race" by creditors, the need for debtor countries to obtain "working capital" when they have suspended their debt-service payments, and the need for finding ways to prevent a small number of dissident creditors from blocking an agreement acceptable to the vast majority of creditors.

The working party rejected the bankruptcy approach, however, not merely because of the huge practical problems involved in reaching agreement on an international bankruptcy code, but also because the basic analogy between domestic and international bankruptcy is flawed. The safeguards against moral hazard built into domestic bankruptcy codes cannot be applied to sovereign debtors. In the working party's own words, "it would be neither appropriate nor possible to replace the authorities responsible for economic policies of a sovereign state with a 'new management,' or to take possession of a state's non-commercial property."

And there is a second objection. The decision of a private debtor to file for bankruptcy is usually forced upon it. The decision of a sovereign state to suspend its debt-service payments is at least partly volitional. It reflects the government's judgment that the economic and political costs of the policy measures required to avoid a suspension, such as a tax increase, exceed the reputational and other costs of a suspension. It is worth noting, in this connection, that no major country, other than the United States, extends the protection of bankruptcy law to subnational governments, and that U.S. law extends protection to municipalities and other local entities but not to state governments.

The working party also considered a laissez-faire approach to the problem—letting debtors and creditors work out their problems without official involvement. This strategy would deal effectively with the moral-hazard problem by making it costly for debtors to suspend debt-service problems and making it costly for lenders to underestimate the risks of a suspension. But the working party rightly rejected this approach as well, stating that "the extent of public concerns likely to be at stake when a liquidity crisis occurs provides sufficient justification for the authorities to look for ways to foster cooperative efforts by debtors and creditors to contend with unexpected payments problems."

The working party was equally clear, however, on one crucial point. Debtor countries and their creditors must not expect the international community to deal with crises by providing massive financial assistance to debtor countries, and no class of creditor should expect to be exempted from a suspension or debt restructuring in the event of a future crisis. The working party made the following recommendations, which constitute a middle-ground approach to sovereign liquidity crises:

First, debtors and creditors should include in sovereign-debt instruments three sorts of contractual provisions: (1) clauses concerning the collective representation of creditors in the event of a crisis; (2) clauses to permit qualified majority voting on proposals to alter the terms of debt contracts; and (3) clauses to require that creditors share all payments actually received from a debtor. The need for collective representation is obvious, and the other two types of clauses will help meet the needs stressed by Sachs and others. Qualified majority voting will prevent dissident creditors from delaying agreements between creditors and debtors. Sharing clauses will discourage creditors from trying to grab assets for themselves.

Second, the working party made a recommendation that will help meet a debtor's need for working capital. When a debtor has been obliged to suspend its debt-service payments and has undertaken to adopt the policies necessary for it to return eventually to creditworthiness, the IMF should be prepared to provide financial support before the country has reached an agreement with its creditors and cleared its arrears. "Such lending," the working party said, "can both signal confidence in the debtor country's policies and longer-term prospects and indicate to unpaid creditors that their interests would best be served by reaching an agreement with the debtor." The ministers and governors of the G–10 countries have endorsed these conclusions and recommendations.

Some will say that the recommendations made at the Halifax Summit and in the report of the working party are inconsistent. The Halifax Communiqué called on the IMF to streamline its procedures for working with countries that need financial assistance to deal with a liquidity crisis, and it called for enlargement of the credit facilities available under the GAB. But the working party warned that creditors and debtors should not count on large-scale official assistance. These recommendations are not inconsistent, however. On the contrary, they speak to the ambiguities and uncertainties that reside in the problem they seek to address. Creditors and debtors must not count on large-scale official assistance, but the need for such assistance cannot be ruled out categorically, and the IMF must therefore have access to adequate financial resources and the ability to provide them rapidly in those rare cases in which they will be required.

Some market participants are likely to say that the recommendations of the working party will make it too easy for borrowers to suspend their debt-service payments and will thus undermine the basic principle that debt contracts must be honored. But market participants have also acknowledged that suspensions can and will occur. The bonds of many developing countries carry rates of return at least 300 basis points higher than those carried by comparable bonds issued by industrial countries. The buyers of those bonds are thus saying that there is even now a nonnegligible risk of total default on those bonds and a correspondingly greater risk of a suspension or partial default. A 300-basis-point premium implies a 3 percent probability of total default in any single year and thus a very much larger probability of total or partial default over the life of a bond. The recommendations of the working party aim at reducing the cost of such defaults, not only to the creditors, but also to the debtor, to other borrowing countries, and to the entire international community.

The working party made one more recommendation that was endorsed by the Lyons Summit in June 1996. It called for efforts to strengthen the financial systems in emerging-market countries so as to reduce the risks they pose in the event of a crisis. The Lyons Summit, in turn, called for the adoption of strong prudential standards in emerging-market countries and urged international financial institutions and bodies to promote the development of effective supervisory arrangements in those countries. The work started by the Halifax Summit will thus continue for some time.

CRISIS MANAGEMENT IN EMERGING CAPITAL MARKETS

William R. Cline

1 From the Brady Plan to Post-Tequila Arrangements

The response of the Group of Ten (G–10) and the International Monetary Fund (IMF) to the Halifax Communiqué should be seen as the next phase in the ongoing evolution of industrial-country financial policy toward developing countries. This policy has evolved from an early emphasis on bilateral aid in the 1960s, to multilateral lending in the 1970s, to private-bank recycling of petrodollars in the mid-1970s (to the delight and relief of the G–7 countries), and to the series of initiatives that managed and eventually resolved the debt crisis of the 1980s. Among these initiatives were initial emergency lending, the indicative-target Baker Plan, and the Brady Plan (Cline, 1989, 1995).

By 1993, the emerging capital market had soared to new heights, marking a post-Brady epoch. The Mexican peso crisis, however, brought a chill to this new market. The official community has responded with a number of initiatives, the driving force of which seems to be the political imperative that Mexico-style bailouts cannot be repeated (given the U.S. political backlash, coupled with some central-banker indignation that Wall Street holders of tesobonos emerged unscathed). What is remarkable about these initiatives, however, is that they are preemptive rather than remedial, in clear contrast to all the debt measures of the previous two decades. Preemptive measures may be seen either as prescient stitches in time or as putative cures that are worse than the probability-weighted disease. Which of the two these emergency measures are will become clear only as they are implemented in practice.

Despite the Mexico crisis, private-capital flows to emerging economies reached a new peak of \$200 billion in 1995 (IIF, 1996a).[1] Argentina, worst hit by the tequila effect, was back in the market by mid-year, as was Mexico itself. It seems likely that the forceful U.S.-IMF financial support of Mexico helped achieve this outcome.

The views expressed here should not be attributed to the Institute of International Finance or its board of directors.

[1] Here and throughout, billion equals a thousand million.

2 Data, Surveillance, and Security Blankets

Everyone agrees on the desirability of one element of the initiative: the IMF's undertaking on standards for data release, including a system for achieving better practices of compliance (IMF, 1996a). These standards are close to those proposed by the Institute of International Finance (IIF, 1995, 1996a). Although it seems likely that improved data availability can help investors make informed decisions—and there could eventually be a spread penalty for a country's failure to release timely data—data improvement can, in contrast to improvements in underlying policies, make only a modest contribution to market stability.[2]

Country surveillance is supposed to address the efficacy of underlying policies. The IMF is understandably unprepared, however, to release to the public its Article IV policy reviews. Because the private market is liquid, moreover, countries increasingly can afford to ignore the IMF and eschew its standby programs, as they did in the 1970s. If there is a new, tougher IMF in print, it is difficult to detect from the institution's premier publication (IMF, 1996b); the most recent issue of the *World Economic Outlook* contains only limited, telegraphic evaluations of a few leading countries in the emerging markets. Although surveillance is increasingly becoming the task of the private sector, most of the country analysis publicly available comes from investment houses, the research divisions of which are, perhaps inherently, subject to influence from their sales divisions.[3]

If the surveillance leg of the new strategy remains shaky, there is the doubling of the General Arrangements to Borrow (GAB) to provide comfort in case things go wrong. I have always been puzzled, however, about the way in which this reform is supposed to help. The GAB is explicitly reserved for cases of systemic crisis and has not been used since 1978, when the United States borrowed funds to help stop the dollar's decline. Given the dominant European view that even the Mexican crisis was not systemic, it is unclear whether the GAB will be of relevance to emerging markets. In other words, the entity now has twice as much money not to lend. In practice, doubling the GAB

---

[2] It is a matter of controversy whether data opacity was a problem in the Mexican case. It may not have been a problem for sophisticated investors with specialized data access. With respect to ordinary investors, however, it is notable that the December 1994 issue of *International Financial Statistics* had reserves data for Mexico only up to July 1994.

[3] An important source of private-sector country analysis is provided by the periodic in-depth reviews and updates on fifty emerging economies conducted by the Institute of International Finance. These country studies are available, however, only to the institute's 200-plus members.

(in part by enrolling newly rich contributors such as Singapore) amounts to insuring against the contingency that IMF quotas will not keep up with lending needs. In that event, the IMF could borrow from the GAB. At least until recently, however, the IMF has had ample excess liquidity, and despite its large loans to Mexico and Russia, a serious resource shortfall does not seem imminent.

In sum, the measures taken so far add up to being helpful at the margin and, in the case of the GAB perhaps, to providing psychological security. Although the data, surveillance, and GAB measures shore up weaknesses in the existing system, they do not radically change it. That is probably to the good.

3 Crisis Management

The other, less tangible but potentially more important, component of the official community's post-Mexico initiatives is the development of strategies for handling Mexican-style crises in the future. A central question in such strategies is whether they are broadly designed around private-sector action or official-sector intervention. A related question is whether crises are resolved on a case-by-case basis or according to prearranged patterns.

The basic choice is thus between a market-based approach that features ad hoc *ex post* action developed by private creditors and the debtor, and a more interventionist approach based on *ex ante* mechanisms orchestrated primarily by the official sector. Before turning to the G–10 proposal (1996), it is useful to consider the analytical framework for addressing the problem, as well as the principles that should underlie a market-based strategy.[4]

Analytical Framework

The theory of sovereign lending holds that because there is no physical collateral that can be seized in sovereign lending, the main assurance the lender has of repayment is the knowledge that default will be painful to the borrower. Correspond-ingly, the more investors perceive that institutional arrangements are trending toward "no-fault default" with minimal pain for the borrower and substantial risk of politicization of debt, the less willing they will be to supply capital to emerging

[4] This strategy, along with consideration of the G–10 proposals, will be set forth in more detail in a forthcoming study by the Institute of International Finance's Working Group on Crisis Resolution.

markets. At the same time, borrower response to the same perception will be to increase the demand for borrowing. Although it is fashionable in policy circles to downplay such borrower moral hazard on grounds that the disruptions of even an officially assisted crisis are severe, country policies come in gradations rather than polar binary alternatives, and the perception that payments may be more eagerly suspended would seem capable of shifting the center of gravity along the policy spectrum.

If this is true, the result would be to reduce capital supply and increase capital demand in emerging capital markets. In Figure 1, the equilibrium volume and interest rate occur where the emerging economies' demand curve for capital (DD) intersects the international financial market's supply curve (SS). Adoption of a formal international mechanism for financial emergencies or debt workouts that are perceived to reduce default penalties will cause the demand curve to shift outward (to $D'D'$) and the supply curve to shift backward (to $S'S'$). The market clearing price of the debt will move upward, from the initial interest rate of R_0 to R_1. The outcome for the volume of capital flow is ambiguous, but it would seem more likely to fall (from K_0 to K_1) than to rise. The overall result is the introduction of an inefficiency into the emerging capital market. This inefficiency may be summarized as the consequence of moral hazard posed by the prearranged workout mechanism.

Some might argue that this result would be desirable, because there is too much money flowing to emerging economies. That view seems unjustified; surely the longer-term view is that preserving capital-market access for emerging economies is essential for global development.

One of the standard arguments for new institutional mechanisms is that the capital market for emerging economies can face market failure because each individual creditor tends to act without considering the negative externalities for others. When there is a run on the country and a fear of default, an "asset grab race" by creditors can cause the country to experience an unnecessarily severe recession. The creditors themselves will thus also suffer from their failure to coordinate and to facilitate a smoother adjustment by the country (Eichengreen and Portes, 1995; Sachs, 1995).

The classic formulation of this problem is the "free-rider" argument. It was precisely a free-rider problem that led to the process of "concerted lending" in the mid-1980s, whereby an advisory committee of large international banks suggested arrangements for rescheduling and for new money. In the context of the 1990s, the argument of free-rider market failure has increasingly been extended to include the difficulty

10

FIGURE 1

DEMAND AND SUPPLY FOR CAPITAL FLOWS TO EMERGING MARKETS

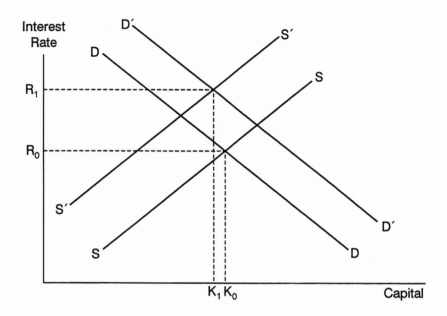

of achieving collective action among large numbers of disparate, perhaps anonymous, bondholders.

Invoking the 1980s free-rider argument in the changed context of
the 1990s markets can be misleading, however. The major banks today
are not vitally endangered by risks from claims on debtor countries, as
they were in the mid-1980s, when such claims were high relative to the
banks' capital. Those banks that still hold the Brady bonds for which
they exchanged their earlier claims are protected by the Brady guarantee mechanisms. The creditor-borrower relationship has thus turned
from symmetric to asymmetric; from vital on both sides to vital for the
debtor but peripheral for the creditor (Truman, 1996). Under these
circumstances, creditors may well judge that there is more to be lost
from submitting claims to official orchestration than from the nonmobi-
lization of free riders. Indeed, rounding up new money is far less
probable today, and the outcome of a crisis is far more likely to be
simply the selling off of claims in the secondary market.

With respect to the salient role the proposed official mechanisms
attribute to internalizing bondholder externalities, three points need to

11

be made. First, bonds remain only a modest part of debt. At the end of 1995, non-Brady bonds represented about 13 percent of the total external debt of emerging economies and about 15 percent if debt owed to multilateral official institutions is excluded.[5] Second, bonds are largely irrelevant for severe and sudden runs on a country's foreign exchange. Bonds have maturities, and holders cannot run unless their maturities have fallen due. If they try to run, they must sell the bonds to others; the net call on the country's resources, or foreign exchange, or both, cannot be accelerated ahead of the bond-principal maturity. Third, many institutional investors in bonds seem more likely simply to sell off their holdings at a loss in the event of crisis, rather than become involved in collective action by bondholders, especially in attempts at concerted new lending.

The discussion of new mechanisms for financial crisis management has tended to invoke implicit scenarios that are similar to either the bond defaults of the 1930s or the Latin American debt crisis of the 1980s. Yet the capital markets of the 1990s are very different. Today, the problem that seems to have dominated policymakers' concerns has much more to do with an isolated foreign-exchange crisis than with a globally generalized default on bonds or bank loans. Exchange crises arise from the coexistence of a misaligned exchange rate with the widespread shift toward capital mobility in the 1990s. Even a fundamentally well aligned exchange rate can come under attack in this environment, as the French experience shows. It would be a mistake to design quasi rescheduling, and especially quasi bankruptcy arrangements, in an attempt to deal with exchange-rate crises. A standstill on sovereign payments, for example, will not prevent a rush of residents to take their money abroad and a concentrated effort by foreign holders of domestic-currency private assets to convert into foreign exchange for remission abroad. Suspension of sovereign payments pending rescheduling would typically provide minimal immediate cash-flow relief during an exchange-rate crisis.

Similarly, it is crucial for policy design to decide whether the next ten or twenty years are likely to resemble the periods of widespread defaults in the 1930s and 1980s or more benign periods. Systemwide collapses that come along every fifty years may not be the most relevant contexts

[5] At the end of 1995, the thirty-one foremost emerging economies together had outstanding external debt in the amount of $1,683 billion, of which $238 billion was owed to multilateral official institutions. Their total non-Brady bond holdings amounted to $215 billion. The Brady bonds of twelve leading restructuring economies had a face value of $147 billion and a market value of $83 billion (IIF Data Base).

dealing with financial crises. If a country is moving close to crisis, secondary-market prices on its obligations are likely to fall, as is its exchange rate. These price movements are signals that the country should immediately take strong adjustment measures. Once a crisis has actually developed, the responses chosen should allow the market to remain flexible. Creditors should be able to sell out their positions, rather than being frozen in them. This market process should serve as a shock absorber for individual creditors, who can thereby make their own choice between risk and return (and liquidity and return), depending on their circumstances. Holders of bank claims or bonds would thus be able to sell them on the secondary market if they preferred to take the loss immediately and perhaps limit future losses.

The market mechanism can also absorb shocks with regard to portfolio equities. Holders of stocks in the country in crisis are likely to encounter a sharp decline in stock prices, an adjustment that means sellers will obtain lower amounts for their holdings and will thus exert less pressure on foreign-exchange availability than is suggested by precrisis levels. The stock-price reductions will also mean that stocks will appear to be more of a bargain, so that other foreign investors may seek to enter the market—or existing holders may decide not to sell.

Secondary market. The flexibility provided by asset-price movement suggests that it will be important to maintain a functioning secondary market in the face of financial crisis. A market-based approach would recognize that in this process, there is likely to be some shift in the composition of claims holders away from the traditional creditors (banks, mutual funds) to holders such as hedge and "vulture" funds specializing in distressed debt. Market observers note that as prices declined during the stresses on emerging markets after the peso crisis, new investors willing to take advantage of bargain opportunities came forward.

Moratorium. The internal logic of the market-based approach dictates that market participants are cognizant that a possible component of a crisis is a temporary moratorium. Such a moratorium would be one entered into by the country, however, rather than one counseled by the international official authorities (contrary to the suggestion by Eichengreen and Portes, 1995); the principal vehicle for resolving the moratorium would be negotiations between private holders and the country, rather than a formula suggested by the official sector.

Such moratoriums would hardly come as a shock to the private market. They are, indeed, implicit in the high spreads (up to several hundred basis points) that some sovereign bonds pay. Investors in these bonds presumably have geographically diversified portfolios and

15

are unlikely to be shocked if one of the countries in such a portfolio enters into difficulties. Without such perceived risk, the market would quickly bid down the spreads these bonds pay.

Exchange controls. The same logic dictates that market participants know that in some circumstances, countries may be forced to impose foreign-exchange controls. This consideration is particularly relevant to holders of local-currency domestic debt of the government in question. Such debt will typically pay a premium incorporating exchange-rate risk, and this premium is likely to rise as the country moves closer to financial crisis. Once again, the principle is higher return at the price of higher risk.

Modest public support, limited public intervention. A market-based strategy would recognize in advance that the massive official-sector support given during the Mexican peso crisis would not be forthcoming and that the private sector, instead, would be expected to bear the main part of the adjustment. Market participants could reasonably expect, however, that the more normal levels of support from the IMF and from multilateral development banks would be forthcoming if the country were to adopt an adjustment program as part of an overall rescheduling agreement.

Nonassumption of private debt. In a market-based approach, private creditors would not assume that their claims on private-sector debtors would be made whole after the fact through assumption by the host government. In principle, the additional risks associated with lending to the private sector would be incorporated into the spreads on the precrisis loans.

Rescheduling as opposed to forgiveness. One of the surprising features of the debate on institutional change has been its intermixing of rescheduling and forgiveness. In the usual formulation of the problem, the high mobility of the capital market of the 1990s is seen as giving rise to sudden exchange crises, thereby necessitating institutional reform. Such crises presumably reflect problems of liquidity, however, rather than fundamental insolvency requiring forgiveness. Fundamental solvency does not change overnight.

The presumption in a market-based approach to crisis management would be that if the private-capital market in a country was highly active as a source of capital inflows before the crisis, that country is far from being insolvent and is therefore primarily in need of a rescheduling of debts upon the outbreak of the crisis, rather than partial forgiveness of them.

16

Representation. The presumption would also be that in the market-based approach, the London Club (with its substructure of advisory committees) would remain the representative entity of bank creditors. With respect to bondholders, for cases in which bonds remain *de minimus*, the bondholders would presumably not be involved. For cases in which the bond stock has grown to significant levels, the logical approach would be to organize a specific bondholders' committee. There have already been instances of private debt for which this has proved feasible—for example, Aeromexico in Mexico.

4 The G–10 Proposals for Crisis Management

The G–10 report on crisis management has three principal features. First, it affirms a market-based approach. Second, it concentrates its attention on bonds and sees their growing importance as posing a problem, because past workout mechanisms have covered only bilateral lending (Paris Club) and bank lending (London Club). Third, it views payments suspension with tacit (but not formal) international official support as a helpful means of forcing creditors to reach workout agreements. With respect to the first feature, the report states that:[7]

> current practices are an appropriate starting point. . . . They are voluntary and make use of market . . . forces (ES, ¶6). . . . the Working Party concluded that its own work should focus on those approaches that build on existing practices and institutions (e.g., those of the Paris and London Clubs) and are designed to work to the greatest possible extent with the grain of the market (¶4).

With respect to the second, it states that:

> the Working Party focused its attention on those forms of debt to private creditors, such as internationally traded securities, that have increased in importance in the new financial environment but that in the past have usually been shielded from payments suspensions or restructurings (ES, ¶1). . . . There should be no presumption that any type of debt will be exempt from payments suspensions or restructurings in the event of a future sovereign liquidity crisis (ES, ¶2).

With respect to the third feature, the report states that:

> a temporary suspension of debt payments by the debtor may be unavoidable as part of the process of crisis resolution and as a way of gaining time to

---

[7] Paragraph references are to the main report unless indicated as being from the Executive Summary (ES).

put in place a credible adjustment programme (ES, ¶2). The Working Party did not consider that it would be feasible to operate any formal mechanism for signalling the official community's approval of a suspension of payments. . . . [Nonetheless] it concluded that it would be advisable for the IMF Executive Board to consider extending the scope of the current policy of lending, in exceptional circumstances, to a country that faces the prospect of continuing to accumulate arrears on some of its contractual debt-service obligations to private sector creditors ["lending into arrears"], in cases where the country is undertaking a strong adjustment programme and making reasonable efforts to negotiate with its creditors (ES, ¶9). . . . Such a policy is intended to prevent failure to reach agreement with creditors from holding up implementation of an adjustment programme. The provision of financial support by the IMF can improve the bargaining position of the debtor substantially (¶94).

In broad terms, the G–10 working party report is judicious in favoring a market-based approach building on existing institutions. In particular, its explicit rejection of the concept of an international bankruptcy court reflects an important accomplishment of the working party deliberations, in view of the counterproductive effects that such a mechanism could have on international capital flows.[8] Nonetheless, the report reveals some sympathy with the basic idea and notes that "many of the same results could in principle be achieved in more informal ways" (¶26).

The report would seem less well advised in its heavy focus on bonds and payments suspensions. It is unclear that rescheduling bonds is the primary missing link in crisis management or that suspending payments on bank loans and bonds will resolve foreign-exchange crises. Broader asset classes are at stake, including government bonds held by residents and an entire range of financial assets that are subject to capital flight.[9] There is also considerable tension between the suspension approach and the principle, also endorsed by the G–10, that market liquidity and market adjustment should be maintained. Moreover, emphasis on strengthening the debtor's bargaining position through lending into arrears raises the risk of moral hazard on the part of the

[8] The report states that "formal insolvency procedures do not appear to be either appropriate or feasible now or in the foreseeable future." It also judges that "The need for additional protection from creditors has not in the past been a serious problem for sovereign debtors. Such debtors have few assets to seize and some of these benefit from sovereign immunity" (¶26).

[9] The rising role of domestic-currency bonds is evident in the recent introduction of J.P. Morgan's Emerging Local Markets Index (1996), which covers ten countries.

debtor and risks reducing the supply, or raising the price, or both, of international capital flows to emerging economies.

It is also unclear that the G–10 can avoid "formal" IMF endorsement of country arrears even if the IMF does not explicitly invoke its Article VIII provisions whereby IMF signatories are obliged to hold "unenforceable" contracts that violate exchange controls imposed by another member country "consistently with this Agreement" (IMF Article VIII.2.b). An alternative, and perhaps more realistic, interpretation is that once the IMF board approves lending to a country that is in arrears to private creditors, it has "formally" sanctioned those arrears.

The report's endorsement of lending into arrears is problematic. IMF policy was historically just the opposite, and only in 1989 did the IMF board revise its strategy.[10] At that time, there was not only a problem of generalized default, but the IMF was also being asked to contribute resources to the official enhancements of the debt-forgiveness instruments (Brady bonds). Some smaller debtors, such as Costa Rica, were perceived as being "strangled" by the banks, which for reasons of precedence were reluctant to restructure prior to concluding negotiations with larger debtors.

It is somewhat curious that the G–10 seeks to widen IMF lending into arrears to include new instruments (primarily bonds) at a time when the international capital market has normalized and relegated generalized default to the past. One might, instead, have expected a reversion to earlier historical practice. Moreover, it is difficult to envision in today's capital market that any single class of past creditors could financially strangle a debtor. Peru, for example, received large inflows of private capital in the first half of the 1990s, even though it did not agree to a Brady restructuring until 1996. Ultimately, of course, a country in a standoff with its creditors has access to automatic refinancing in the form of arrears, so financial pressure by creditors has its limits. What is of concern is that implicit official international sanctioning of arrears could contribute significantly to the dynamics of moral hazard and capital-market erosion discussed above. Furthermore, the G–10's qualification that the country would have to be "undertaking a strong adjustment programme" is no guarantee that moral hazard would be eliminated. Forceful adjustment can coexist with aggressive

---

[10] The traditional position on arrears was stated in a board decision in 1970; the revised position was stated on May 23, 1989 (IMF, 1995, pp. 127, 356–358).

forgiveness demands, as the cases of Poland and Peru in the early 1990s illustrate. The G–10 report itself reflects the division of viewpoints within the official community on lending into arrears. The report qualifies such lending as limited to "exceptional circumstances" and fails to clarify whether lending into arrears can be expected to be an integral part of most workouts or, instead, to be rarely employed.

A fact sheet given to the press by the U.S. government illustrates the possible management of a crisis. The sequence includes country consultation with the IMF and, if possible, private creditors; IMF and creditor-government determination whether there is a threat to the international financial system; initial corrective macroeconomic measures by the country; suspension on certain types of debt; recognition that such suspension may require exchange controls; IMF and creditor-government action to protect third countries from contagion; estimation by IMF staff of any "financing gap"; an IMF lending program, possibly into arrears; and eventual return of the country to the capital market at higher spreads.

This sequence suggests an approach that may be outmoded. The calculation of financing gaps seems of limited relevance to present-day markets and implicitly invokes the mounting of concerted lending packages. Today, sell-offs in the secondary market (and the corresponding buy-ups by third parties such as hedge funds) are more likely. Current-account gaps are of less relevance when there is the potential for much larger capital outflows under capital mobility (which was typically absent in the debt workouts of the 1980s). The sequence also reveals a concern that the international financial system will be frequently threatened. It is questionable, however, that any emerging-market borrower will be large enough to be a threat, subsequent to Mexico and the lessons learned by the market.

The report recommends that bond clauses provide for rescheduling with nonunanimous vote, the sharing of proceeds among creditors, and the collective representation of bondholders. It suggests, however, that these provisions should be developed by the market rather than be legislated. Nonetheless, it states that "encouragement and support from the authorities can be helpful" (¶62) and cites the precedent of standardization of swaps and other derivatives.

The position that the market should develop its own practices on bondholder councils and rescheduling clauses is important, because official imposition of such conditions for bondholders would tend to curb the market and raise spreads. The evidence so far seems to be that the large mutual funds would eschew *ex ante* bondholders' councils for fear that, as prominent members, they would be "sitting ducks" for official pressure to hold onto a country's bonds in a crisis. With respect to nonunanimous contract revision, some bonds issued in the U.K. market already have such clauses.

The report cites as desirable properties of crisis management that "it should not cause excessive social, political, or economic stress for the debtor," that burdens of "exceptional financing" should be "shared fairly among and across different classes of creditors," and that "governments [should] resist pressures to assume responsibility for external liability of their private creditors" (¶17). Specifically, there should be a "ranking in debts in terms of servicing on their original terms," and "the commitment to ongoing provision of new credits could be one factor in determining which debts are serviced on time" (¶21). This mid-1980s formulation of burden sharing seems anachronistic in view of the greater likelihood of secondary-market disposition (and its imposition of burden sharing through creditor loss) than of the entrance of new money. The explicit statement on "political or economic stress," moreover, is an outright recognition that official orchestration would indeed politicize the resolution of debt crises.

The report contains an appendix reviewing the results of a survey of private-market participants. It acknowledges that many of those surveyed support an alternative approach that would "let debtors and creditors work out problems on their own, without any official involvement whatsoever." The report notes that this private-sector view "appears to be rooted in the suspicion that this intervention may tilt the balance too much in favour of the debtor" and thereby "raise the cost of funds to borrowers [and] narrow the investor base" (¶33).

It should be noted that no support "whatsoever" is an extreme formulation. The more central private-sector view is that normal amounts of IMF standby and other such official support would be fully appropriate in crisis management, but that extraordinary official support analogous to that provided to Mexico would not be expected by the private sector. Similarly, the private sector does not purport to insist that there can be no rescheduling whatsoever. Instead, the point is that if rescheduling occurs, it should be the consequence of discussion between the private creditors and the debtor, rather than a solution formulated by the IMF or another official entity.

The report effectively rejects the noninterventionist view of market participants on grounds that it is "influenced by their expectation that the official sector would in fact continue to play a very significant role [and that] the necessary liquidity would be provided by the official sector,

21

especially in the most severe cases" (¶34). In other words, the G–10 seems to be suspicious that the private sector expects large official bailouts, just as the G–10 believes the private market is suspicious that the official sector will tilt the bargaining in favor of the debtor.[11]

The report recognizes that in all crises, economic adjustment programs are crucial and will usually involve "tightening of monetary policy, a credible fiscal package and possibly some exchange-rate action [that] will help to stem capital flight" (¶72). The report tends, however, to identify adjustment programs as inherently linked to reschedulings and even suspensions. It thereby misses a central class of crisis management (one hopes the dominant class), the forceful adjustment that makes it possible to avoid rescheduling and suspension.

The report sees the central element of a workout as "some appropriate combination of financing or rescheduling," necessitated by the fact that "excessively rapid adjustment may have unacceptably high economic, social, and political costs or may simply not be feasible" (¶73). This is the only place where the report implies that its crisis-management mechanism refers to rescheduling, rather than forgiveness. Although there is no explicit mention of debt forgiveness in the report, the G–10 does not explicitly state that its mechanism would be inappropriate if extended to requests for forgiveness.

The most explicit statement of the rationale for official intervention is as follows: "The aims of the official sector . . . are to minimise systemic risk, to contain contagion, to address market failure and to restore prosperity to the debtor countries" (¶75). If systemic risk and contagion are unlikely, as seems probable given the capital market's relatively sophisticated adjustment to the Mexican peso crisis, then the core questions concern market failure and debtor prosperity. The G–10 assumes that the need for government to orchestrate collective action is the dominant remedy for market failure. However, it is possible that the mechanism set up for this purpose can create market failure of its own of a different type, by creating moral hazard and eroding the confidence of investors. If so, then the question is whether the possible benefits of dealing with the first type of market failure in the crises that do arise outweigh the costs imposed by the second type on the market at large. Similarly, in addressing debtor prosperity, it is important to distinguish between the short term and the medium to long term.

[11] The G–10's presumption that the private sector still expects large bailouts in the future is directly contradictory to the view expressed in one important statement of the position of major creditors (Dallara, 1996).

The report "strongly endorses" the principle of timely payment according to contract but "recognizes that in certain exceptional cases the suspension of debt payments may be part of the crisis resolution process" (¶83). The G–10 working party usefully distinguishes between suspension of interest as opposed to principal, and it notes that "missed interest payments are viewed more negatively by the market" (¶87).

The closest the report comes to recognizing that crises may have much more to do with a generalized run on the currency than with the burden of medium-term debt, and that the solution may have more to do with market mechanisms than with the debt-rescheduling arrangements of the past, is in a section that recommends exchange-rate flexibility rather than exchange controls:

> [There may be] a "rush for the exit" by holders of claims, including domestic holders, who have come to believe that the suspension of payments on their claims can be expected soon. In the case of marketable claims, however, sales may be discouraged by sharp falls in prices caused by the expectation that controls will be imposed; this effect can be reinforced by a depreciation of the domestic currency [and] exchange-rate flexibility could help to conserve the country's remaining foreign exchange reserves and may even obviate the need to obstruct the servicing of the private sector's obligations (¶88).

5 Conclusion

Despite its verbal endorsement of a market-based strategy, the G–10 report risks working against, rather than with, the grain of the market by its emphasis on official orchestration of debt workouts and, especially, its seeming willingness to make lending into arrears an integral part of the strategy of crisis management. The G–10 working group states that cases of lending into arrears "should remain rare, [because they] expose the official sector to the risk that the debtor will not be able to implement its adjustment programme and [they will] thus increase the risks associated with the extension of official assistance. Lending into arrears should therefore always be conditioned on very strong adjustment efforts" (¶93). Yet the report also recommends extending the scope of IMF lending into arrears to classes of debt not now covered—mainly bonds. Extension of this practice is "intended to prevent failure to reach agreement with creditors from holding up implementation of a Fund programme. [This will] improve the bargaining position of the debtor [and] flag to the unpaid creditors that their interests are best served by quickly reaching an agreement with the debtor" (¶94). The G–10 itself thus seems to confirm explicitly the private creditor suspicions that official intervention will "tilt the balance" of negotiations (¶33); the only question is whether it will do so "too much."

In operational terms, much will depend on the way in which the G–10 implements this strategy. If financial crises are few, perhaps one or even two moderate-sized cases a year, and if the G–10 formulation is taken verbatim and any episodes of lending into arrears are assumed to be "exceptional," then defining "exceptional" as no more often than one-fifth of the time would yield, over a five-year period, no more than two cases of lending into arrears. Under such a scenario, neither the private sector nor the borrowing countries would necessarily expect lending into arrears to be a standard feature of a workout. In that case, something not unlike the market-based approach to financial crises might develop.

If, instead, the exception becomes the rule, and practically any financial crisis quickly transits to a payments standstill backed by IMF lending into arrears, the moral-hazard effects of signaling ease of country default, undermining private-sector confidence, and inducing generalized increases in lending spreads to emerging markets will be a likely consequence.

References

Cline, William R., "The Baker Plan and Brady Reformulation," in Ishrat Husain and Ishac Diwan, eds., *Dealing with the Debt Crisis*, Washington, D.C., World Bank, 1989, pp. 176–196.

———, *International Debt Reexamined*, Washington, D.C., Institute for International Economics, February 1995.

Dallara, Charles H., Letter to the Chairmen of the Interim and Development Committees of the International Monetary Fund and World Bank, April 1996.

Eichengreen, Barry, and Richard Portes, *Crisis? What Crisis? Orderly Workouts for Sovereign Debtors*, London, Centre for Economic Policy Research, 1995.

Franks, Julian, "Some Issues in Sovereign Debt and Distressed Reorganizations," in Barry Eichengreen and Richard Portes, *Crisis? What Crisis? Orderly Workouts for Sovereign Debtors*, London, Centre for Economic Policy Research, 1995, pp. 87–102.

Group of Ten (G–10), *The Resolution of Sovereign Liquidity Crises: A Report to the Ministers and Governors*, Basle, Bank for International Settlements, and Washington, D.C., International Monetary Fund, May 1996.

Institute of International Finance (IIF), *Improving Standards for Data Release by Emerging Market Economies*, Washington, D.C., Institute of International Finance, September 1995.

————, "Capital Flows to Emerging Economies and Prospects for 1996," Washington, D.C., Institute of International Finance, May 1996a.

————, *Data Release Standards for Emerging Economies: An Assessment of Country Practices*, Washington, D.C., Institute of International Finance, April, 1996b.

International Monetary Fund (IMF), *Selected Decisions and Selected Documents of the International Monetary Fund*, Washington, D.C., International Monetary Fund, June 1995.

————, *Standards for the Dissemination by Countries of Economic and Financial Statistics: The Special Data Dissemination Standard*, Washington, D.C., International Monetary Fund, April 1996a.

————, *World Economic Outlook*, Washington, D.C., International Monetary Fund, May 1996b.

J.P. Morgan Securities, "Introducing the Emerging Local Markets Index (ELM I)," New York, J.P. Morgan Securities, June 24, 1996.

Sachs, Jeffrey, "Do We Need an International Lender of Last Resort?" Frank D. Graham Memorial Lecture, Princeton University, April 1995, processed.

Truman, Edwin C., *"The Risks and Implications of External Financial Shocks: Lessons from Mexico,"* International Finance Discussion Paper No. 535, Washington, D.C., Federal Reserve, January 1996.

MANAGING THE NEXT MEXICO

Barry Eichengreen and Richard Portes

The Mexican crisis was an extraordinary event that elicited an extraordinary response. The panic that erupted at the end of 1994 threatened the complete collapse of Mexico's banking system and public finances, with dire consequences for economic and political stability. It confronted industrial-country policymakers and officials of the International Monetary Fund (IMF) with a difficult choice. One option was to let events run their course and to allow the Mexican government, its resources depleted, and under pressure to prop up the banking system and the economy, to default on its debts. This would have undermined confidence in other Mexican investments, led panicked investors to flee from the peso and the Mexican banks, and forced the Mexican government to impose exchange and capital controls. During the lengthy negotiations that would have followed, Mexico would have been barred from international capital markets. Investors, painfully burned, would have shied away from other developing countries, and economic liberalization and reform would have suffered a setback not only in Mexico but throughout the developing world.

The other option—and the one that was ultimately pursued—was large-scale foreign aid. Foreign financial assistance allowed the Mexican authorities to keep debt service current and to retire their foreign-currency-indexed debts from the market. Restoring confidence avoided a further collapse of the peso exchange rate that would have pushed more Mexican firms into receivership and raised the level of unemployment. Foreign assistance allowed the public finances to be stabilized and the Mexican government to return to international capital markets in a matter of months.

But the bailout, which enabled Mexico to retire its dollar-indexed debt and let the holders of those securities off without penalty, also encouraged investors to take more risks.[1] Lenders will be tempted to lend, irrespective of risk, if they anticipate another bailout, and governments will be encouraged to pursue risky financial strategies. The

---

[1] This point is emphasized by Meltzer (1995) and Ackerman and Dorn (1995), who argue that it would have been better to let the crisis run its course.

26

handling of the Mexican crisis thus sets the stage for future problems in Latin America and elsewhere in the developing world.

There is thus a need for a third strategy—for another option for managing future Mexicos. This was recognized by the Group of Seven (G–7) at the Halifax Summit in June 1995, where the assembled heads of state and government encouraged the G–10 finance ministers and central bankers to consider new procedures for the orderly resolution of sovereign-debt crises. The G–10, in response, established a working party comprising representatives from the ministries of finance and central banks and chaired by Jean Jacques Rey, deputy governor of the National Bank of Belgium (Halifax Summit, 1995).[2]

That group has now come forth with its recommendations (G–10, 1996). These include changes in the provisions of loan contracts, including possibly clauses authorizing the formation of bondholders' steering committees and permitting the IMF to lend into arrears. For the most part, however, the report delegates responsibility for action to the markets. It encourages the markets to incorporate new clauses into loan contracts but, for fear of upsetting investors, does not encourage the G–10 governments to be actively involved. To avoid any hint of interfering, it says nothing about the need for government accreditation of bondholders' committees. It urges the IMF to consider lending into arrears but does little to provide the necessary finance; specifically, it fails to endorse an increase in IMF quotas or to clarify the terms of access to the General Arrangements to Borrow (GAB). This cautious approach, adopted in reaction to the skepticism of market participants, leaves the world dangerously exposed to future crises.

And more such crises will occur, as they always have. Mexico in 1994–95 is only the latest in a long sequence of such episodes, in the 1830s, 1850s, 1870s, 1890s, 1930s, and 1980s. That crises recur is no surprise, because periodic financial difficulties are actually a sign that the international capital market is functioning well. If no firm ever declared bankruptcy, the capital market would be failing at its job. Profitable investment opportunities sometimes become unprofitable because of unanticipated events. At that point, the company in question has to declare bankruptcy, and its operations are liquidated or reorganized. That is how an efficient capital market works. If there

---

[2] Although the G–7 issued the call for the creation of a study group, the G–10 formed it, because the General Arrangements to Borrow (GAB) is a creation of the G–10, and it is possible that its resources will be drawn upon in a future crisis. A parallel group was created to study the enlargement of the GAB.

were no bankruptcies, we would infer that lenders were so risk averse as to be missing profitable investment opportunities.

The same applies to countries. Governments have risky investment opportunities that should more than repay foreign investors, in an expected value sense, for the cost of their funds and for bearing risk. Sometimes, however, those investments fail, and countries find themselves in a position analogous to that of bankrupt firms. This is a normal, indeed a healthy, outcome when it occurs in response to unanticipated events, and it is precisely why one should think that the Mexican crisis is not one of a kind. Thus, although it is desirable to provide more information to the markets and to make every effort to avert foreseeable crises, such measures will never eliminate the need for orderly procedures to pick up the pieces when things go wrong.

1   The Matter with Mexico

Even if the pattern is predictable, particular events are not. Individual crises in financial markets are, by their nature, unanticipated. This was certainly the case in December 1994. Neither the markets nor policy-makers saw the Mexican crisis coming, and neither had contingency plans.[3] Investors, having believed that the exchange rate was locked and that the Mexican government's debts were as solid as U.S. Treasury bonds, reacted with horror to the devaluation of the peso and to the failure of the new government of Ernesto Zedillo to prepare for the event. They scrambled to liquidate their Mexican securities, and the peso quickly lost half its value. This meltdown placed the country's financial system and ten years of economic reform at risk (Sachs, Tornell, and Velasco, 1996).

Not only in Mexico were officials caught off guard. The governments of the leading creditor countries also lacked procedures for responding to a crisis in an emerging market. The IMF was the obvious vehicle for lending assistance, but normal procedures required that a loan be preceded by the negotiation of a stabilization program, a task that might be impossible to complete before the Mexican government was forced into default and the country's banking system collapsed. The assistance that could be rendered was ostensibly limited by Mexico's IMF quota, the size of which had been set so as not to strain the Fund's

[3] A number of commentators (Williamson, 1993; Dornbusch and Werner, 1994) noted the need for a devaluation of the peso, but none anticipated the financial crisis that would follow.

resources. The General Arrangements to Borrow, under which the industrial countries stood ready to assist one another in the event of difficulties with their finances, had never been intended to address the problems of a developing economy; as originally constituted, only a contributing country could draw on it. In response to the debt crisis of the early 1980s, however, non-G–10 countries were permitted access in the event of an "exceptional situation of a character or aggregate size that could threaten the stability of the international monetary system."[4] One can argue, with the benefit of hindsight, that the Mexican crisis threatened the stability of emerging markets worldwide, but this was far from clear at the time. Even had it been clear, the GAB's caretakers might still have insisted that instability limited to developing countries did not constitute a threat to the international monetary system and hence did not qualify for support. This was certainly the predominant view among European officials at the time (Bergsten and Henning, 1996).

Under pressure of time, governments and international organizations scrambled to react. Lacking another strategy, they could only throw money at the problem, and even this was not done in an orderly way. The Clinton administration initially attempted to assemble a $40 billion U.S. support package on its own.[5] Evidence that it would be unable to push aid of this magnitude through the Congress then forced the administration to take recourse to the Exchange Stabilization Fund (ESF), a reserve that had been set up some sixty years earlier to support the dollar against foreign currencies—not to support foreign currencies against the dollar.[6] The ESF could provide only $20 billion, however, leading the administration to enlist the help of the IMF, the Bank for International Settlements (BIS), and governments in Europe and Japan, and to solicit a contribution from the commercial banks. The IMF responded favorably, offering the Mexican government an unprecedented $17 billion, roughly seven times the country's quota. The European and Japanese governments, however, objected to not having been consulted or informed. They agreed only reluctantly; indeed, several European countries abstained out of pique on the initial IMF vote on the Mexican package.[7]

---

[4] The GAB members themselves had to satisfy a somewhat less demanding test, that of forestalling or coping "with an impairment of the international monetary system."

[5] Here and throughout, billion equals a thousand million.

[6] The ESF had, in fact, been used earlier to support the peso (Schwartz, 1996).

[7] Some observers suggest that the United States hesitated to consult its G–7 partners precisely because it anticipated a negative response (Bergsten and Henning, 1996). The BIS topped up the loan to $52 billion, but the commercial banks declined to contribute.

The American approach can be defended on the grounds that it would have been even more costly for governments to do nothing. A full-blown financial meltdown, culminating in the suspension of debt-service payments, would have interrupted Mexico's access to foreign capital for an extended period (DeLong, DeLong, and Robinson, 1996). It could have discredited the government's program of economic reform and jeopardized the results of more than a decade of liberalization. An even more serious depression than actually occurred might have destabilized Mexico's political system and, coming in the wake of the North American Free Trade Agreement (NAFTA), discredited the proponents of trade liberalization in the U.S. Congress. Had Mexico closed itself off from international markets, and the bad old days of slow growth returned, there might have been unprecedented immigration into the United States.[8] Investors, having been burned once, would have shunned emerging markets. The crisis could thus have spilled over to other developing countries, destabilizing conditions in Argentina and elsewhere where the hold of economic reform was still tenuous.

Even those who accept these arguments will admit that the bailout of Mexico gave rise to moral hazard. Although containing one crisis, it increased the likelihood of another. Whatever the G–10 governments may say now, the markets know what they did last time. They know that governments will be under the same severe pressure to bail them out the next time around.

The circumstances will be different, however. The Mexican bailout provoked a harshly negative reaction in the U.S. Congress. Wall Street interests were seen as advocating a policy that allowed the Mexican government to retire the assets of foreign investors and financial institutions at full value courtesy of the American taxpayer. Drawing on the ESF antagonized the Congress, which saw this as a way of avoiding the need for its advice and consent. Members of Congress called for the suspension of the aid program and proposed legislation to bar the Treasury from again using the ESF under similar circumstances.

All this makes it unlikely that there will again be a U.S.-led rescue of a country in Mexico's position. The U.S. Treasury's freedom of action will be limited. Crises farther from U.S. borders will lack the same salience in Washington, D.C., and neither European nor Japanese governments are likely to regard instability in emerging markets as sufficiently threatening to spearhead a Mexico-style rescue.

[8] There is reason to think that worries about migration were more than posturing. Hanson and Spilimbergo (1996) find a large elasticity of illegal migration with respect to the peso-dollar exchange rate.

2 The Emergence of Emerging Markets

The Mexican crisis was possible only because significant changes had occurred in the international financial markets. In the first half of the 1990s, capital flowed to developing countries in unprecedented amounts. Private flows to developing countries averaged $1.2 billion a year between 1961 and 1970 and $3.8 billion a year between 1971 and 1980 (Cuddington, 1989). Following the "lost decade" of the 1980s, lending exploded. Aggregate net long-term resource flows to developing countries rose to $46 billion in 1990, $103 billion in 1992, and $173 billion in 1994 (World Bank, 1995). This flow of funds had an important impact on the recipient countries. In the Mexican case, net capital inflows averaged 6 percent of gross domestic product (GDP) in the first half of the 1990s.

This surge of capital to emerging markets reflected four factors. Most fundamental was economic liberalization and reform in the developing world. Developing countries emerged from the debt crisis of the 1980s with a firmer grasp on fiscal conditions and with inflation increasingly under control.[9] Consumer-price inflation in Latin America, excluding Brazil, fell to 14 percent in 1994, down from 1,400 percent in 1989. Latin America's fiscal balance moved from deficits of nearly 10 per cent of GDP in 1988 to close to balance by the early 1990s (Eichengreen and Fishlow, 1996).[10] The ethos of liberalization encouraged the deregulation of domestic markets, foreign trade, and capital transactions. Tariffs were reduced, encouraging trade-related inward investment. Privatization created new opportunities for financial capital. The economies of East Asia survived the debt crisis unscathed and moved up the technological ladder toward the production of higher value-added goods. It is hardly surprising that investors were attracted to opportunities in the developing world.

The second factor encouraging capital transfer was financial deregulation. By the late 1980s, both industrial and developing countries had begun deregulating their financial markets. Trade liberalization had made capital controls more difficult to enforce: importers and exporters

[9] Our discussion focuses on Latin America and East Asia, which were the principal destinations for portfolio capital in the early 1990s. Other regions, including South Asia, China, Eastern Europe, and Africa, where systematic economic reform was initiated at a later date, were slower to receive large amounts of foreign capital, although in some cases, inflows have recently reached high levels.

[10] The Mexican fiscal deficit, which with interest payments had accounted for 12.5 percent of GDP in 1988, moved strongly toward balance as early as 1990 (Velasco and Cabezas, 1996).

could overinvoice and underinvoice transactions and exploit "leads and lags" to circumvent restrictions on capital flows. New information technologies and the globalization of financial markets made the regulations and restrictions needed to close off domestic financial markets more costly and onerous still; it was hardly possible to deregulate banking systems while continuing to prohibit banks from borrowing and lending abroad. Encouraging the development of a stock market as a way of capturing financial business from regional rivals and offering domestic firms a cheap and attractive source of external finance was an uphill battle so long as foreign investors were barred from participation.

The debt reduction afforded by the Brady Plan also helped to set the stage for the explosion of capital flows to the middle-income developing countries that had previously been caught in the debt crisis. Between 1990 and 1993, countries participating in the Brady Plan were able to reduce their debt loads by 10 to 20 percent by exchanging their floating-rate bank debt for bonds that bore below-market interest rates and by discounting the original loan (Dooley, Fernandez-Arias, and Kletzer, 1996, table 1).[11] This deal was attractive to the banks, which had concluded that government bonds were less risky than bank loans to private and sovereign entities. The subsequent rise in the secondary-market prices of commercial bank debts suggests that the markets perceived a significant improvement in the creditworthiness of these countries. It is no coincidence, in light of what followed, that Mexico was the first country to make use of the Brady Plan.

But economic conditions in the borrowing regions do not provide a complete explanation for the surge in capital flows. Countries such as Peru and Brazil received substantial inflows even before making significant progress toward macroeconomic stabilization or completing Brady Plan operations. This points to a fourth factor encouraging lending to emerging markets: monetary policies in the creditor countries. Capital flows to emerging markets are extraordinarily sensitive to the level of global interest rates. Lower rates in the financial centers stimulate investors to search for yield abroad, and they enhance the creditworthiness of developing-country borrowers by reducing the cost of servicing existing debts. Thus, the debt loads of developing countries were cut not only by the Brady Plan, but also by the effect declining world interest rates had on the cost of servicing their floating-rate debts.

[11] The principal amount of the defaulted loans was typically reduced by 35 to 50 percent, whereas accrued interest was generally not reduced. Brady bonds were collateralized with U.S. Treasury (zero-coupon) bonds.

These effects were evident, starting in 1989, when short-term U.S. interest rates trended downward, coincident with the resurgence of foreign lending. The U.S. rates were reduced by the Federal Open Market Committee, which sought to stimulate recovery from the recession of the early 1990s and to counteract the weakness of the California economy. By 1994, when it was clear that recovery was secure, the Federal Reserve turned its attention to inflation and raised interest rates. It thereby increased the yield and attractiveness of domestic securities but heightened the debt-servicing burdens of countries such as Mexico, which had substantial short-term obligations outstanding.[12]

As important as the magnitude of these flows, however, was their composition. In the 1970s, lending had been directed primarily at governments, private foreign borrowing in developing countries still being tightly controlled. In the most recent episode, in contrast, capital inflows were directed overwhelmingly at the private sector. The World Bank's figures suggest that two-thirds of all lending from 1978 to 1981 went to the public sector, but that between 1990 and 1993, more than 80 percent of all long-term private capital received by developing countries flowed to the private sector (Fernandez-Arias and Montiel, 1996, table 3). Although the line between private and public debts is not easy to draw, what with the implicit guarantees that governments extend to parastatals and private enterprises, the shift in composition is clear.

In the 1970s, bank loans and direct foreign investment had been the principal conduits for private-capital transfer to emerging markets. Starting in 1989, the volume of securitized investment exploded. The use of bonds and other securities as vehicles for redistributing financial capital internationally was particularly important for developing countries. The volume of foreign capital that flowed into the bond markets of developing countries rose by a factor of ten between 1989 and 1993. Investment in emerging stock markets rose in parallel during the period, again by a factor of ten. Unlike the direct foreign investments that had dominated the industrial countries' private investment in the developing world for much of the postwar period and the bank loans that had provided the vehicle for capital transfer in the 1970s, these

[12] Calvo, Leiderman, and Reinhart (1992), Chuhan, Claessens, and Mamigni (1993), Fernandez-Arias (1994), and Dooley, Fernandez-Arias, and Kletzer (1996) all conclude that fluctuations in international interest rates account for a sizable share of the recent variation in capital flows. One may wish to argue further, following Krugman (1995), that financial markets overreacted to the cut in interest rates in the industrial world. Although we do not view this as an essential part of the story, it reinforces our point.

stocks and bonds were highly liquid; they could be sold as easily as they had been purchased. Capital flows could now turn on a dime.

3 Wild Bourses

The Mexican meltdown revealed four problems with this market structure. First, investors in liquid securities have an overpowering incentive to scramble for the exits when confronted with uncertainty. Like depositors who join their neighbors outside a bank to liquidate their holdings before the bank's cash reserves are exhausted, investors in government bonds have an incentive to liquidate their holdings when others do because they grow fearful that the government's limited foreign-exchange reserves will be exhausted. This is what happened in 1994 when holders of Mexican cetes and tesobonos rushed for the door.[13]

Second, a government experiencing a debt run, like a bank experiencing a run by its depositors, may have no choice but to suspend payments, regardless of the damage to its creditworthiness. On the eve of the Mexican crisis, the government of Mexico was responsible for more than $18 billion of dollar-denominated and dollar-indexed liabilities, an amount roughly triple its foreign-exchange reserves. Once investors began to liquidate their holdings, the authorities were at their mercy.[14]

Third, it can be exceedingly difficult to restructure debts—to convert and extend their terms of payment. Bondholders are unsure how much the government is able to pay. Governments are unsure how much the bondholders are willing to accept. And both sides have an incentive to withhold information to win bargaining points. On top of this problem of strategic behavior between the creditors and the debtor are the conflicts among different classes of creditors. Altering the core terms of a bond covenant normally requires the unanimous consent of the bondholders, which can be all but impossible to obtain. Individual investors will be tempted to refuse any offer of less than a hundred cents on the dollar in the hope of being bought out at full value by the government or other creditors. Small creditors seeking a favorable deal can thus hold up the settlement process indefinitely.

[13] The phenomenon of self-fulfilling bank runs has been modeled by Diamond and Dybvig (1983). Sachs, Tornell, and Velasco (1996) and Cole and Kehoe (1996) translate the problem to the case of a government and its creditors.

[14] In principle, a government in this position could restore investor confidence by raising interest rates on its debts. In practice, however, higher interest rates might so weaken the public finances and the domestic economy as to be insupportable.

Fourth, in this climate of uncertainty, potential providers of additional liquidity will hold back. Lenders will hesitate to provide new money for fear that it will be garnished by old creditors. The government and the country will be starved of finance for even highly productive investments.

These problems already existed in the 1980s, when commercial banks were the conduits for capital transfer. Then, too, negotiations complicated by imperfect information and brinkmanship could take many years to complete. Small banks held their larger counterparts hostage, rejecting settlement offers until they were bought out at full value. Providers of new money held back so long as unpaid creditors stood ready to garnish all resources on which the government could lay its hands.

The problems are even more serious now that securitized instruments have replaced bank loans. There were never more than 750 banks involved in sovereign-debt reschedulings during the 1980s, and bank advisory committees rarely had more than a dozen members. The largest banks could demand discipline of their smaller counterparts, threatening to exclude renegades from future loan syndicates and to otherwise undermine their position within the banking community if they refused to cooperate. Pressure was also applied by the U.S. government, which feared that the debt crisis could jeopardize the stability of the financial system. These efforts to secure a quick resolution were, nevertheless, only modestly successful. Problems of collective action and strategic behavior, however significant then, are many times greater now. Today, there exist thousands of small bondholders whose consent is required to restructure the core terms of loan contracts. The prevalence of bearer bonds makes it difficult even to identify the owner, much less to apply peer pressure. The incentive for any one investor to provide new money to kick-start the debtor's economy is further diminished when all creditors are small relative to the market. It is revealing that the IMF attempted to coordinate the provision of private financing for countries in arrears early in the debt crisis of the 1980s but made no similar effort in 1995.

4 An International Bankruptcy Court?

A provocative proposal for coping with financial crises in emerging markets came from Jeffrey Sachs (1995a, 1995b), who advocated an international bankruptcy court (see also Cohen, 1989). Sachs appealed to the analogy with Chapters 9 and 11 of the U.S. Bankruptcy Code, under which the liabilities of municipalities and corporations in financial distress are liquidated and restructured. In the domestic context, these statutes attempt to balance the sanctity of loan contracts against the need to restore the economic viability of overindebted enterprises. The enforcement of debt contracts is important because, in its absence, creditors will refuse to lend. Clearing away unserviceable debts is desirable if doing so facilitates the survival of a firm the assets of which are worth more in place than when dismantled and distributed piecemeal to the creditors.

A well-designed bankruptcy procedure balances these two desiderata. It does so by permitting the courts to impose a standstill that halts the creditors' scramble to seize the firm's remaining assets, which could otherwise shut the firm down. If the enterprise is viable, its liabilities are reorganized and its operations restructured under the supervision of an officer of the court, who works in concert with management and the creditors. Important to this process is "cramdown," which allows the court to force minority claimants to accept the restructuring plan subject to the consent of specified majorities of different classes of creditors. To facilitate the injection of the liquidity the firm needs to restructure and maintain operations, bankruptcy procedures generally assign seniority to new money.

To apply Chapter 11 at the international level, Sachs advocated the establishment of a bankruptcy court for sovereign debtors. Such a body would be empowered to declare a standstill, negotiate a debt restructuring, promote adjustment by the debtor country, cram down settlement terms, and inject catalytic finance. The G–10 working party quickly, and correctly, concluded that this idea was a nonstarter. Private creditors would be reluctant to forego their recourse to national courts in return for the creation of an international tribunal. The main effect of creating a world court empowered to restructure sovereign debts would have been to alarm investors and raise the cost of borrowing to developing countries.

Investors had good reason to be alarmed by such proposals, because the moral hazard created by a sovereign bankruptcy procedure would be great—greater than in the domestic setting. National courts can throw out the management of a firm entering receivership. They can seize its assets and distribute them to the creditors. Such threats induce shareholders to monitor management and limit irresponsible borrowing, and they deter management from using bankruptcy strategically—from walking away from their debts when they are able to pay. These sanctions would not apply to governments, however. Gunboat diplomacy being a thing of the past, governments cannot be "replaced" in the way that courts replace the management of bankrupt firms. Exports can be routed through third markets to prevent their seizure. Governments possess few assets offshore that can be attached by their creditors, even where international law might permit it, and some assets, like the foreign reserves of national central banks, are protected by the sovereign-immunity laws of countries like the United States and the United Kingdom.[15] All this makes it unrealistic to think that there could ever be an international bankruptcy court.

5 Market Fears or Market Paranoia?

The working party had to steer around not only the overly ambitious proposals of academics but also the unsympathetic reactions of practitioners. As background to its deliberations, the G–10 surveyed market participants in the principal financial centers. The overwhelming consensus was that existing arrangements should be left unchanged. Market participants asserted that any attempt to develop new institutions and procedures for resolving sovereign-liquidity crises would alarm the markets and raise the cost of finance to developing countries. Their argument was that default should be as messy and painful as possible in order to protect the sanctity of loan agreements. Changes that make debt workouts easier are undesirable because they will encourage governments to repudiate their debts. Procedures that facilitate workouts and writedowns would thus leave lenders reluctant to lend. They would increase the cost and reduce the availability of funds, to the disadvantage of borrowers as well as lenders.

Preserving the sanctity of loan contracts is not, however, the sole objective of the social institutions of the market. Measures to ensure the enforceability of contracts must be balanced against the need to restore the economic viability of overindebted enterprises and economies. The argument for making workouts as painful as possible, taken literally, implies abolishing domestic bankruptcy laws, something no sensible observer would propose. One could, of course, go further and recommend capital punishment for bankrupts! That would certainly discourage insolvency, but it would be neither efficient nor socially acceptable.

It is not unreasonable that portfolio managers are more concerned with their bottom line than with the Mexican economy, or that they dismiss the idea that there can be exceptional circumstances under

---

[15] The governments of debtor countries have sought to invoke sovereign immunity more widely, although the courts in both the United States and the United Kingdom have been moving away from a strict interpretation of the law.

which their contracts must be modified by *force majeure* for the good of society. What is more surprising is that they overlook the fact that there are circumstances under which mechanisms to restructure debts efficiently will work to the advantage of the creditors themselves. Where incomplete information and collective-action problems impede restructuring, removing them can avoid an extended period during which negotiations are stalled, no interest is paid, and productive investment opportunities go unexploited. We would not expect the abolition of domestic bankruptcy laws to improve the market terms for corporate borrowers, after all. Efficient restructuring arrangements can increase the size of the pie available for distribution to the debtors and creditors, leaving both better off. This is why we allow the intervention of courts in domestic bankruptcy proceedings, and why the G–10 has now put forward modest proposals for facilitating restructurings of sovereign debt.

6   The G–10 Recommendations

Governments are already able to impose the essence of a creditor standstill by declaring a moratorium on payments.[16] The G–10 report acknowledges the need for temporary suspensions of payments, observing that these may be "unavoidable as part of the process of crisis resolution and as a way of gaining time to put in place a credible adjustment programme" (G–10, 1996, p. i). And it stresses that no class of creditors (with bondholders specifically in mind) should regard its claims as so sacred as to be exempt from this prospect.

Normally the IMF has provided finance only after negotiating a program with a country and after the latter has cleared away its arrears. It has typically waited for agreement with the Paris Club and the bank steering committee, although there have been exceptional cases in which it has gone ahead when the debtor has arrears with commercial banks that may continue to increase. These have been cases in which prompt support has been deemed to be essential for the implementation of an effective adjustment program and in which negotiations with the creditors have been expected to yield an agreement in good time. The G–10 report suggests that the IMF extend this practice to debts owed to other private creditors, including bondholders, in cases in

---

[16] Although governments are still subject to legal harassment when they take this step, foreign courts have, as explained above, only limited ability to enforce their judgments.

which the country is undertaking a strong adjustment program and making a reasonable effort to negotiate with its creditors.

The report concludes that it is not feasible for the IMF to protect countries from the consequences of a moratorium by endorsing the government's decision to declare one.[17] But lending into arrears will have much the same effect. In addition to providing catalytic finance to jump-start the debtor's economy, it will signal the creditors that their interests are best served by reaching an agreement with the debtor.

To facilitate the process of restructuring sovereign debts, the G–10 proposes modifying the provisions of loan contracts to incorporate a "collective-representation clause" designating the creditors' representative and making provision for a bondholders' meeting.[18] It recommends incorporating clauses that allow the core terms of bond contracts to be altered without the unanimous consent of the holders. Decisions reached by such qualified majority vote would bind all creditors, eliminating the ability of a small minority to block a restructuring until they are bought out by other creditors or the debtor government. It recommends the addition of sharing and nondiscrimination clauses similar to those that have traditionally been included in the loan agreements of bank syndicates. Specifying that additional payments obtained by any creditor would have to be shared with the entire class will diminish the incentive to hold up a settlement.[19]

The G–10 portrays its proposals as complementing efforts to strengthen crisis prevention. It recommends enhancing IMF surveillance, improving the quality and timeliness of data on external debt, and fortifying financial systems in developing countries in an effort to avert crises before they occur. The IMF (1996), for its part, is considering more regular reviews of economic conditions and policies in individual

---

[17] In Eichengreen and Portes (1995), we recommended that the IMF be more forthright in its opinion of the advisability of a country's unilateral suspension as a way of shielding governments from the negative reputational effects of suspensions taken in response to disturbances beyond their control.

[18] International bond issues do make provision for an agent (typically called the fiscal agent), who does not represent the bondholders in negotiations but is authorized to call meetings and issue notices. Many sovereign-bond agreements, most notably Brady bonds, do not provide for bondholders' meetings even at the initiative of the bondholders or the debtor (Macmillan, 1996).

[19] The report recommends limiting sharing clauses to individual bond issues, rather than applying them to all of the country's creditors, as a compromise between the desire to promote creditor cohesion on the one hand and avoid cumbersome communication problems on the other.

countries and has indicated its intention to encourage the timely publication by governments of economic statistics by announcing publicly which countries satisfy its standards for data dissemination.

7 The Need for Government Intervention

Better data and surveillance are admirable, but they are not enough. Crises can still erupt for reasons that are neither easily anticipated nor readily averted. Prevention may be the better part of cure, but there is still the need for intensive care when the patient takes ill.

The G–10 proposes to meet this need through a "market-driven process" of contractual reform. Governments are to trumpet the virtues of clauses providing for bondholder representation, qualified majority voting, and the sharing of information, but to otherwise take no action; they are to hope that the markets will see the light. This is as unrealistic as the academic calls for an international bankruptcy court. If contractual changes were so easily adopted, the markets would have embraced them already. There would be no need to recommend action.

There are significant obstacles to market-driven reform. For one thing, different countries, because of different national traditions, provide for the organization and representation of bondholders in different ways. To the extent that national practices differ, underwriters of international bond issues have been unable to agree on an arrangement that is not off-putting to a particular set of national clients.

Even if financiers and governments could agree on a universal set of contractual reforms, the organizational costs of implementing them would still have to be overcome. Consider the ban on majority voting to restructure the core terms of loan agreements. Even if everyone would be better off under a majority-voting scheme, changing the current regulatory structure would be costly, and no individual debtor or creditor would be inclined to shoulder those costs, because the probability of having to invoke the provision on a particular bond issue would be so slight. These considerations lend a strong element of inertia to existing contractual provisions (Roe, 1996).

Finally, there is the "prenuptial agreement" problem. If only some sovereign borrowers include a qualified-majority-voting clause in their loan agreements, creditors may suspect that those debtors anticipate having to restructure in the not-too-distant future. The clause will therefore be taken as a negative signal, rendering investors reluctant to lend.

If such clauses are to become widespread, all countries—even the advanced industrial nations whose creditworthiness is well established—

40

will have to adopt them. Similarly, the governments of the leading creditor countries may have to guide underwriters to a particular set of model clauses to surmount the obstacles posed by different national traditions and to overcome the costs of altering existing regulatory structures. The changes in contractual provisions recommended by the G–10 must therefore be promoted by enabling legislation. The U.S. Trust Indenture Act of 1939 could be modified to allow the fiscal agent or trustee to take a more active role in representing bondholders in restructurings. Similar legislation would have to be adopted in the other principal creditor countries, such as the United Kingdom, where the fiscal agent is also used. The addition of sharing clauses to all sovereign bonds subject to national law could be mandated by legislation. The G–10 report, in the desire to look "market friendly," however, is silent on the need for legislation. At one point, it acknowledges the existence of the first-mover problem, but it quickly dances away from it.

Although noting that bondholders have organized representative committees in the past and suggesting that this is an appropriate way of solving the representation problem, the report does not recommend that the G–10 governments promote the establishment of a standing committee for this purpose.[20] The argument for a standing committee is that arranging representation on the spot can be difficult and costly, thereby prolonging negotiations. History has shown, moreover, that in the absence of official intervention, a confusing proliferation of committees can spring up. Fly-by-night operators have an incentive to offer representation to investors in the hope of earning a commission in return for negotiating a settlement. This was the state of affairs until the Corporation of Foreign Bondholders was recognized as the representative of British bondholders in the 1890s and the Foreign Bondholders Protective Council received the endorsement of the U.S. State Department in the 1930s.

---

[20] Some members of the G–10 working party may have anticipated that defaulted debts will be bought up by "vultures," whose small number will allow governments to negotiate with them relatively easily. The working party may have had in mind the example of the Dart family, which bought up more than $1.38 billion of Brazilian debt and engaged in extensive negotiations with, and litigation against, the Brazilian government from 1994 to 1996. Although such a scenario is possible, given sufficient time, the process of consolidating bond holdings in the hands of a small number of investment professionals will not be completed in a matter of days or months. In the absence of a representative committee authorized to speak for the bondholders, negotiations will remain messy for some time. Again, the working party may have erred on the side of inaction in order to appear as noninterventionist as possible.

8 IMF Bailouts

The G–10 sends mixed signals about the prospects for large-scale financial aid in the event of future crises. Its statements recommend generally against such large-scale emergency financing as the $50 billion Mexican package, suggesting that other governments should not expect to receive comparable assistance. Its actions, however, betray a willingness to contemplate emergency financing. Encouraging the IMF to lend into arrears when a country has an adjustment package in place will give the IMF increased scope for extending financial assistance, assuming that its managing board authorizes the G–10 recommendation. At its autumn 1995 meeting, the interim committee of the IMF endorsed the establishment of a new standing emergency-financing mechanism (EFM) under which borrowers will be provided with faster access to IMF arrangements and larger up-front disbursements. Documents will be circulated to members of the Fund's executive board, and decisions will be reached with unprecedented speed. To finance the operation of this mechanism, the G–10 and other countries have negotiated a doubling of the GAB.

For cases in which a country already has appropriate economic policies in place, a loan from the IMF may be all that is needed to repel the threat to its financial stability. The danger, of course, is that the IMF and the G–10 will also rely on financial assistance under other, less appropriate, circumstances. If no steps are taken by governments to encourage the adoption of new provisions in loan contracts and to accredit bondholders' representative organizations, the G–10 will rely too much on financial assistance and too little on debt restructuring. Insofar as institutional obstacles to restructuring remain, the only option will be to throw money at the problem. Officials may find that even an expanded GAB is not enough, and that the IMF's new quick-disbursing mechanism does not disburse with sufficient speed. Doubling the GAB from $27 billion to $54 billion or more is not insignificant, but it is unimpressive in the context of the $52 billion put together for Mexico or the $30 billion that the IMF alone has committed to Mexico and Russia. It also remains to be seen whether access to the GAB will be liberalized. All this suggests that providing the necessary finance will require raising IMF quotas. Desultory discussions about a quota increase in 1997–98, in the interim committee and elsewhere, need to give way to prompt action.

9 The Prospects for Action

The G–10's proposals, if adopted, would be a positive step. They will not be adopted, however, without action as well as words from governments. It is essential that the advanced industrial countries and the developing countries in strong financial positions push for the G–10 proposals and that they support parallel initiatives to enlarge IMF quotas. The Clinton administration, if not necessarily the Congress, is likely to support expanded financial resources for the IMF, because the United States is the leading source of portfolio capital to emerging markets and is the country that underwrote the largest share of the Mexican bailout. The proposals have some support in the IMF as well, where they are seen as a way of expanding the organization's influence and raising its profile.

The other high-income countries may not agree, however. The German authorities are preoccupied by moral hazard and worry that any reforms will encourage reckless lending and overborrowing. The Japanese, remembering their own experience with bank insolvencies, feel much the same way. The French and Italians worry that an agreement to rewrite international-debt contracts will force them to do the same for their parastatals. And the most prosperous and financially secure developing countries, which were not consulted by the G–10, may be suspicious of innovations that acknowledge the possibility, however slight, that debts might one day have to be restructured. The debate will therefore pit the United States and the IMF against reluctant partners in both the public and private spheres, just as the Mexican meltdown did in 1995.

Institutional reform to better cope with future crises will therefore require strong leadership from its supporters and an effective campaign to win over the financial community. Otherwise, the next crisis may so hurt market participants that they will voluntarily agree to reforms far more radical than the modest proposals of the G–10 report. The G–10 would do well to recall the experience of the League of Nations' committee established in the aftermath of the sovereign-debt defaults of the 1930s. That committee also recommended changes in loan contracts to enhance bondholder organization and representation (League of Nations, 1939). In the absence of anything other than a statement of desirability by the League, however, there was no response at all by the markets. There is reason to fear that the same will happen again.

References

Ackerman, Paul, and James A. Dorn, "Dose of Financial Morphine for Mexico," *Financial Times* (London), February 15, 1995.

Bergsten, C. Fred, and C. Randall Henning, *Global Economic Leadership and the Group of Seven*, Washington, D.C., Institute for International Economics, 1996.

Calvo, Guillermo A., Leonardo Leiderman, and Carmen M. Reinhart, "Capital Inflows to Latin America: The 1970s and 1990s," Washington, D.C., International Monetary Fund, 1992, processed.

Chuhan, Punam, Stijn Claessens, and Nlandu Mamigni, "Equity and Bond Flows to Latin America and Asia: The Role of Global and Country Factors," Policy Research Working Paper No. 1160, Washington, D.C., World Bank, July 1993.

Cohen, Benjamin J., "A Global Chapter 11," *Foreign Policy*, 75 (Summer 1989), pp. 109–127.

Cole, Harold L., and Timothy J. Kehoe, "A Self-Fulfilling Model of Mexico's 1994–95 Debt Crisis," Staff Report No. 210, Federal Reserve Bank of Minneapolis, Research Department, 1996.

Cuddington, John T., "The Extent and Causes of the Debt Crisis of the 1980s," in Ishrat Husain and Ishac Diwan, eds., *Dealing with the Debt Crisis*, Washington, D.C., World Bank, 1989, pp. 15–42.

DeLong, J. Bradford, James DeLong, and Sherman Robinson, "The Case for Mexico's Rescue," *Foreign Affairs*, 75 (May/June 1996), pp. 8–15.

Diamond, Douglas, and Phil Dybvig, "Bank Runs, Deposit Insurance and Liquidity," *Journal of Political Economy*, 91 (June 1983), pp. 401–419.

Dooley, Michael, Eduardo Fernandez-Arias, and Kenneth Kletzer, "Recent Private Capital Inflows to Developing Countries," *World Bank Economic Review*, 10 (January 1996), pp. 27–50.

Dornbusch, Rudiger, and Alejandro Werner, "Mexico: Stabilization, Reform and Growth," *Brookings Papers on Economic Activity*, 1 (1994), pp. 253–316.

Eichengreen, Barry, and Albert Fishlow, "Contending with Capital Flows: What is Different About the 1990s?" Occasional Paper, New York, Council on Foreign Relations, January 1996.

Eichengreen, Barry, and Richard Portes, *Crisis? What Crisis? Orderly Workouts for Sovereign Debtors*, London, Centre for Economic Policy Research, 1995.

Fernandez-Arias, Eduardo, "The New Wave of Private Capital Inflows: Push or Pull?" Policy Research Working Paper No. 1312, Washington, D.C., World Bank, June 1994.

Fernandez-Arias, Eduardo, and Peter J. Montiel, "The Surge in Capital Inflows to Developing Countries: An Analytical Overview," *World Bank Economic Review*, 10 (January 1996), pp. 51–80.

Group of Ten (G–10), *The Resolution of Sovereign Liquidity Crises: A Report to the Ministers and Governors*, Basle, Bank for International Settlements, and Washington, D.C., International Monetary Fund, May 1996.

Halifax Summit, "Communiqué," June 15–17, 1995.

Hanson, Gordon H., and Antonio Spilimbergo, "Illegal Immigration, Border Enforcement, and Exchange Rates," National Bureau of Economic Research Working Paper No. 5592, Cambridge, Mass., National Bureau of Economic Research, May 1996.

International Monetary Fund (IMF), "Standards for the Dissemination by Countries of Economic and Financial Statistics," discussion draft prepared by a staff team, Washington, D.C., International Monetary Fund, 1996.

Krugman, Paul, "Dutch Tulips and Emerging Markets," *Foreign Affairs*, 74 (July/August 1995), pp. 24–44.

League of Nations, *Report of the Committee for the Study of International Loan Contracts*, Economic and Financial Series 1939.II.A.10, Geneva, League of Nations, 1939.

Macmillan, Rory, "Towards a Sovereign Debt Work-Out System," forthcoming in *Northwestern Journal of International Law and Business* (1996).

Meltzer, Allan H., "A Mexican Tragedy," Carnegie Mellon University, 1995, processed.

Padoa-Schioppa, Tommaso, ed., with Michael Emerson, Kumiharu Shigehara, and Richard Portes, *Europe After 1992: Three Essays*, Essays in International Finance No. 182, Princeton, N.J., Princeton University, International Finance Section, May 1991.

Roe, Mark J., "Chaos and Evolution in Law and Economics," *Harvard Law Review*, 109 (May 1996), pp. 641–668.

Sachs, Jeffrey D., "Alternative Approaches to Financial Crises in Emerging Markets," Harvard University, Harvard Institute of International Development, December 1995a, processed.

——, "Do We Need an International Lender of Last Resort?" Frank D. Graham Memorial Lecture, Princeton University, April 1995b.

Sachs, Jeffrey D., Aaron Tornell, and Andrés Velasco, "Lessons from Mexico," *Economic Policy*, 22 (April 1996), pp. 13–64.

Schwartz, Anna J., "The Mexican Loan Repayment Sleight of Hand," in Shadow Open Market Committee, *Policy Statement and Position Papers*, Public Policy Studies Working Paper Series No. 96–01, University of Rochester, Bradley Policy Research Center, 1996, pp. 95–105.

Velasco, Andrés, and Pablo Cabezas, "Dealing with Capital Inflows: Mexico and Chile Compared," New York University, April 1996, processed.

Williamson, John, "Exchange-Rate Policy in Mexico," Testimony to the U.S. House of Representatives, Committee on Small Business, May 20, 1993.

World Bank, *World Debt Tables*, Washington, D.C., World Bank, 1995.

CRISIS PREVENTION AND MANAGEMENT: LESSONS FROM MEXICO

Arminio Fraga

1 Background

Many excellent analyses of the Mexican crisis of 1994–95 are now available (for example, Calvo, 1995; IMF, 1995a, 1995b; Leiderman and Thorne, 1996). My goal here is not to supersede these discussions, but to add, instead, the viewpoint of someone who lived (perhaps I should say survived) the crisis as a market participant. I hope the Wall Street analysts quoted below will appreciate having their anonymity protected.

At the end of 1993, after a decade of extraordinary progress, the Mexican economy was finally ready to take off. The country was run by a competent team of U.S.-trained technocrats, most of whom had already occupied important positions in the previous administration. Continuity was not seen as a problem, because everyone expected that another president from the Institutional Revolutionary Party (PRI) would win comfortably and cleanly after the preceding decade's successes. The North American Free Trade Agreement (NAFTA) was just around the corner, bringing with it a promise of smooth convergence toward the standards of the north.

The Mexican story was, indeed, a good one. After the debt crisis of 1982, Mexico produced an astonishing fiscal turnaround of more than 10 percent of gross domestic product (GDP), progressing from a primary budget deficit of 2.5 percent of GDP in 1982 to a surplus of 4 percent in 1983 to a peak primary surplus of 7.9 percent of GDP in 1989. Inflation control was achieved through an agreement on incomes policy (*Pacto*) that supplemented strict monetary and fiscal policies with wage, price, and exchange-rate targets and guidelines. Results were impressive, with inflation declining from triple-digit annual rates in 1987 to single-digit rates by 1993. The macroeconomic policies were, in turn, accompanied by structural reforms aimed at transforming Mexico into a full-fledged market economy. These reforms included privatization, deregulation, trade liberalization, and financial reform.

From the standpoint of financial markets, the Mexican story was not only a good one, it was also exceptionally well told. Mexican officials were remarkably adept at explaining their program, and one could hear

46

exactly the same presentation, in perfect English, from just about anyone who mattered in Mexico, including spokesmen from the private sector. Indeed, it was not even necessary to go to Mexico, for well-planned road shows were constantly touring the world's main financial centers. As one very influential and credible observer wrote in June 1993, after hearing the Mexicans, "It isn't just that Salinas says all the right things; it's the way he handles himself, the way he responds to tough questions, the caliber of his senior ministers. Pedro Aspe may be the best finance minister around. Over the years, I have met the government officials of many developing countries, and I think that this Mexican government is the best I have seen anywhere." Another analyst asked in a much publicized piece in May 1993 whether "Mexico is still an emerging market," and concluded that "Mexico appears to have emerged." Reactions of this kind help to explain the large capital inflows that more than financed the substantial current-account deficits that Mexico was accumulating from 1991 to 1994.

By 1993, however, some analysts (including those quoted above) were beginning to add a few caveats to their assessments, noting that Mexico's economy was neither growing much nor saving much. In fact, they noted that national saving had declined, from 21.6 percent of GDP in 1987 to 14.1 percent of GDP in 1993, and that the current-account deficit approached 7 percent of GDP as early as 1992. The main warning at the time came from Dornbusch and Werner (1994, p. 253), who argued that "the stabilization strategy has led to an overvaluation of the exchange rate, a precarious financial situation, and a lack of growth. Real interest rates paid by firms continue to be very high, non-performing loans have been increasing, and the current account deficit stands at more than $20 billion."[1]

Yet the basic argument that the Mexican officials were competently spoon-feeding to market analysts was still working. My mid-1993 notes from a meeting with a senior government official tell me that it went as follows: stable macroeconomic plus structural reforms *will* deliver growth. Productivity is up despite the slowdown ("you see, exports are growing at double-digit rates again, so there is no serious overvaluation"). The one-time consumption boom is over. Mexican industry is modernizing fast ("some sectors will just have to disappear, so our rate of growth, itself an average, does not do justice to the progress we have made"), and NAFTA will bring in the foreign direct investment necessary to reduce the dependence on short-term external financing. In fact,

[1] Here and throughout, billion equals a thousand million.

47

Mexico is one of the very few countries in the world (none of which are in Europe) that satisfies the very strict Maastricht conditions [Q.E.D].

Some observers took a then-popular approach, arguing that given a fiscal surplus, one need not worry about a current-account deficit driven by private decisions. Their reaction was motivated by the widely accepted view that the debt crisis of the 1980s had been driven primarily by the loose fiscal policies of the debtor countries.

Another important warning had been issued even earlier by Calvo, Leiderman, and Reinhart (1993), who had pointed out that a substantial portion of recent capital inflows into developing countries was the result of external factors (such as an expansionary U.S. monetary policy) that could reverse themselves. This view attracted very little attention at the time it appeared, but its conclusions are critical to understanding the events of 1994–95. One cannot look at the bust of 1994 without also examining the boom of 1993. Just as the extraordinary global bull market of 1993 was in large part a consequence of the low interest rates prevailing in the United States during that year, the worldwide bond-market crash of 1994 followed from the tightening that began in the United States early in 1993. The impact of this reversal on the ability of the borrowing countries to finance their current-account deficits was visible to the naked eye. Mexico was the worst hit country, but it was by no means the only country affected.

2   1994: A Brief Postmortem

After a disappointing 1993, Mexico went into 1994 looking for an economic recovery to guarantee victory for the PRI in the upcoming presidential elections. Then, two quite different shocks hit Mexico. The first was an internal one-two punch: the Chiapas revolt in January followed by the Colosio assassination in March. Mexico, which had been seen as a model of political and social stability, was suddenly seen as a country with complex social problems and a history—recently discovered—of political instability.

At the same time, the U.S. Federal Reserve began what would be a year-long process of monetary tightening in the United States. The impact of this tightening on global markets was nothing short of spectacular. Bond markets worldwide woke up from a dream of ever-falling long-term interest rates, and leveraged buyers scrambled for the narrow exits in an attempt to preserve their fast-shrinking capital. In this environment, the less liquid and more speculative securities suffered the most. Spreads on the Mexican par bond (the 6.25 percent

Brady bond) went from 300 basis points over U.S. Treasuries to a high of 650 basis points in mid-April. Shortly thereafter, the Colosio assassination triggered the first significant run on the peso, a run that caused the exchange rate to jump to the weak side of the band (a depreciation of some 10 percent) and reduced foreign-exchange reserves from $28 billion to $17 billion—a loss the magnitude of which was not known exactly at the time.

The Mexican authorities reacted by allowing interest rates to rise (the interbank reference interest rate rose from 10.8 percent in February to 22.1 percent in April) and by starting to substitute tesobonos (dollar-linked bills) for cetes (peso bills). This was designed as a display of strength, because it implied that Mexico was committed to a strong-peso policy. Still, these policies were insufficient to prevent an expansion of central-bank credit, which offset the monetary contraction associated with the loss in reserves.

Market analysts remained somewhat optimistic about Mexican prospects, arguing that "Mexico does not need devaluation to boost export competitiveness" (May 3, 1994) and that, with no fiscal deficit, no NAFTA, and so on, "this time is different" (August 22, 1994). Some did suggest, however, that there were difficulties, pointing out that the March "depreciation reflected the opposite movement in the stance of U.S. and Mexican monetary policies as business-cycle conditions diverged. Mexico was struggling to reactivate its economy in time for the election. . . . [The] Banco de Mexico reduced the interest rate on 28-day cetes by 500 basis points to 8.8 percent by the end of February. During this period, short-term interest rates in the United States increased 50 basis points" (May 3, 1994). Observations of this sort were typically followed, however, by constructive remarks stating that tight fiscal and monetary policies and a PRI victory in the presidential elections would see Mexico through the exchange-rate pressure. A few analysts who were less optimistic stated that "prospects for slow growth in 1995 imply pressure to change exchange-rate policy, even before the new administration [takes office]" (July 22, 1994). After April, however, the markets calmed down, and after the successful election of President Zedillo in the beginning of August, they settled even more.

It subsequently became clear that Mexico had not tightened its policies but had, rather, promoted an expansion of credit through the official development banks that reached 4 percent of GDP by the end of the year. In the United States, moreover, the Federal Reserve was not done with tightening. Mexico's reserves stopped falling temporarily during the second and third quarters, but issues of tesobonos during those months accounted for an increasing part of the financing for the current-account deficit, which had now reached 8 percent of GDP.

At that point in 1994, Mexico was no longer the darling of the foreign investor. All of a sudden, it was seen as a country with a crowded schedule of short-term foreign borrowings needed to cover the growing current-account deficit, a deficit that, in turn, was the product of a declining rate of saving and an overvalued currency. The final attack on the peso came in the fourth quarter of 1994 and was probably triggered by rumors that the incoming administration was re-evaluating the exchange-rate policy and by the assassination of Ruiz-Massieu, the secretary general of the PRI. All this helped to crystalize the perception that the new *Pacto* signed on September 28, 1994, would not be sufficient to deal with Mexico's financial problems in a world environment of shrinking liquidity. Once again, the central bank's reaction was to defend the peso by drawing down foreign-exchange reserves. Domestic interest rates were allowed to increase somewhat, but with a weak banking sector, there was clearly a limit beyond which the Banco de Mexico would not be willing to tighten. Anecdotal evidence now suggests, in fact, that Mexican banks were among the first to cover their peso exposures. Mexico was on a slippery slope, with no way to stop.

Table 1 summarizes the changes in the pattern of Mexico's external financing during the crisis period. It shows that the major change occurred in the availability of private financing, which, for the reasons stated above, dried up during 1994. The important role of local capital flight is reflected in the increase by nearly $5 billion in resident lending. The sequence of events probably entailed a gradual and continuous slowdown in foreign financing followed by a burst of capital flight. Note also that foreign equity investment (direct and portfolio) did not decline during 1994.

TABLE 1

EXTERNAL FINANCING IN MEXICO, 1993–1995

(*in billions of U.S. dollars*)

	1993	1994	1995
Current account	−23.4	−29.4	−0.7
Foreign equity investment	15.1	15.1	7.5
Borrowing from foreign official sources	−0.9	0.2	24.5
Borrowing from foreign private sources	21.1	7.8	−13.3
Resident lending to foreigners	−4.1	−9.0	−4.9
Reserve loss	−6.9	18.4	−9.6

SOURCE: IIF, *Mexico Country Report* (1996).

3 1995: Crisis Management

Mexico's first reaction to the crisis was to put together a package of measures designed to support a discrete devaluation of the peso. The program was presented at the Federal Reserve Bank of New York on December 21, 1994, by the new finance minister of Mexico, in office just a few weeks. Senior U.S. government officials were present at the meeting but did not address the hostile audience. The reactions of the market participants gathered there were highly emotional, perhaps indicating that the turbulence was only beginning. Although the program presented included most of the ameliorative policies that Mexico would, in fact, adopt during 1995, the angry crowd was in no mood to listen. One participant even went so far as to yell, "you promised you would never devalue the peso!" a promise that had, indeed, been made. The announced one-time shift in the exchange-rate band lasted only one day. After that, the Banco de Mexico had to allow the peso to float freely.

Market concerns at that time had already shifted from devaluation risk to default risk. Direct peso exposure in the financial system was minimal, so attention turned to the ability of Mexican dollar borrowers, including the Mexican government, to fulfill their obligations. In particular, many observers questioned the ability of the Mexican government to service or to roll over the heavy concentration of tesobono maturities coming due in the first half of 1995.

The initial program included an $18 billion line of credit from the U.S Exchange Stabilization Fund, which would have bolstered the approximately $6 billion in reserves that Mexico still held. Two weeks latter, under additional market pressure, the proposed financing package was increased to $40 billion in loan guarantees and other mechanisms. Markets challenged the package as not fully feasible, however—because the package required congressional support, which seemed uncertain at the time—and thus possibly insufficient to cover all of Mexico's short-term obligations ($10 billion in tesobonos coming due in the first quarter, plus the off-shore funding of Mexican banks, most of which had borrowed aggressively in the period coming up to the crisis). The exchange rate quickly reached the rate of 6 pesos per dollar, a level that clearly overshot any rational estimate of a "needed" devaluation.

Market participants became obsessed at this point with estimating Mexico's short-term cash needs, generally assuming that only a small fraction of the maturities coming due would be rolled over. Mexico's years of fiscal prudence and its beautifully low debt-to-GDP ratio became irrelevant, as everyone wondered whether Mexico could make the next payment. As the end of February approached, another run on

51

the peso threatened to develop, and the exchange rate climbed right through the 6 to 1 level. This time, the United States offered a more credible credit line of $20 billion and, more significantly, Mexico signed an agreement with the International Monetary Fund (IMF) for a line of credit in the unprecedented amount of $17.8 billion. This new package was to be completed by a bridge loan of $10 billion from the Bank for International Settlements (BIS)—some arm-twisting of unhappy Europeans was probably required for this—and $3 billion in credits from commercial banks—which never came through. By the time doubts about the legal details of the agreements and the timing of disbursements were resolved, the peso had briefly touched 7.75 pesos to the dollar on March 9, before finally stabilizing at about 6 pesos in April.

The figures for Mexico's external financing from 1993 to 1995 (Table 1) tell a clear story. Private foreign sources of capital (debt plus equity) declined from $36 billion in 1993 to –$6 billion in 1995, a shift equal to 10 percent of Mexico's GDP. Mexico was able to avoid defaulting on its external obligations thanks only to an extraordinary domestic adjustment, which almost eliminated a current-account deficit of 8 percent of GDP in one year, and to an equally extraordinary financing effort from official sources of $25 billion. The domestic costs of the adjustment, however, were extreme. GDP declined by 6.9 percent in 1995, and inflation reached 52 percent.

One final aspect of "crisis management" was tied to the reversal in U.S. monetary policy in July 1995. The 25-basis-point cut in the Federal Funds rate signaled the end of the period of tightening liquidity and cleared the way for a resumption of capital flows to emerging markets and a recovery in asset prices.

4   Some Lessons

With perfect hindsight, we can now say that the Mexican crisis was the product, as such crises always are, of an unfortunate combination of shocks (domestic and external) to a vulnerable economy. The lesson Mexico learned during the debt crisis of the 1980s was that external borrowing to finance budget deficits is not a good idea. Although the Mexican government's fiscal behavior was exemplary this time around, external borrowing was nevertheless still used unwisely, to finance consumption instead of investment. This point is easily quantifiable. From 1987 to 1994, Mexico's current account dropped from a surplus of 2 percent of GDP to a deficit of 8 percent of GDP. During the same period, gross domestic investment increased by only 2 percent of GDP (IMF, 1995a, p. 92).

One sign that borrowing may be excessive is that it becomes too concentrated on short maturities. Indeed, an important lesson of history (and not just Mexico's history) is that excessive short-term borrowing should not be used to cope with emerging balance-of-payments problems. It should be noted, however, that excessive short-term borrowing is a sufficient condition for crisis vulnerability, but not a necessary one. In markets where derivative instruments are available—where market participants can sell a currency short using forwards, futures, swaps, options, and other instruments—participants other than those who hold outright short-term claims on a country can put great pressure on its currency simply by taking short positions. This was not an important factor in the Mexican case, because formal and informal restrictions imposed by the Mexican government made it difficult to sell the peso short.

How can countries avoid excessive short-term borrowing? The causal relationships are frequently misunderstood in this respect. Countries that invest more tend to have better access to long-term funding. High investment rates, for example, are generally associated with higher imports of capital goods, which typically come with long-term financing. Countries that consume more, however, tend to have difficulty attracting long-term funds. Countries that find themselves in this position should change their policies in order to avoid potential crises.

But countries do borrow short term and continue to do so even when faced with difficulties of a more fundamental nature. Why do they do this? It may be because politicians in many instances operate with horizons that are shorter than those of society (for example, their mandates). This possibility would seem to justify the introduction of institutional restrictions on a government's ability to borrow more short-term debt. Although such restrictions would make sense, they would not constitute a panacea, any more than independent central banks can offer a guarantee against inflation and other financial problems. Indeed, Mexico's central bank was given formal independence at the end of 1993, but in the pressure of an election year, it still felt the need to accommodate a weak banking sector.

If Mexico is thought to have borrowed too much, it is also fair to ask why the markets were so lax in providing the financing. Having asked the same question about the debt crises of the 1930s and 1980s (Fraga, 1986), I would answer again that investors behave myopically, each one perhaps thinking that it will be possible to exit ahead of the rest. Moral hazard on the part of investment bankers (who hope to earn underwriting fees) and of Wall Street traders and mutual-fund managers (who are paid bonuses every year) also helps to explain the Mexican case.

In 1994, however, and contrary to common belief, lack of information does not seem to have been a major problem. There is no question that better information makes markets more efficient. Furthermore, the weak liability structure produced by Mexico's balance-of-payments financing was not well understood by investors, and better disclosure could have reduced the supply of funds sooner. The IMF's initiative to set standards for the dissemination of economic and financial data is in this respect timely and most welcome. Improvements in government and financial-sector liability data would be particularly useful, because they would allow for the construction of aggregate-debt profiles for countries as a whole.

It is nevertheless hard to argue that the proposed new standards would by themselves have avoided the Mexican crisis or have even made it less violent. In the 1990s, unlike the 1930s and perhaps the 1980s, when total debt exposures were unknown, most of the relevant data necessary for a diagnosis of the Mexican situation was available to the general public. It was made available, moreover, according to a schedule that was respected by the Mexican government even during the crisis. Most of the complaints voiced by the market after the run on the peso had to do with the data on foreign-exchange reserves (released three times a year) and on the provision of credit by the official development and trade banks (unavailable at the time). Had the data on reserves been available in real time, however, markets would have panicked earlier and, perhaps, a little less.

At this point, I am forced to conclude that better disclosure of country data and stronger economic institutions (such as independent central banks and more transparent budgetary practices) can reduce the chances of another Mexican crisis but cannot totally prevent it. It is therefore crucial that the potential lenders of last resort, such as the Group of Ten countries and the multilateral institutions be prepared to face future crises. Unlike the domestic case, for which accepted central-banking principles suggest that a central bank lend freely against good collateral, there is no collateral in international sovereign lending. The decision to support a country in trouble has thus to be well founded and based on the best possible information. In particular, not every country should be bailed out. This suggests the need for a close and permanent relationship between the IMF and potential borrowers. The IMF should, in fact, act as the permanent auditor of countries, which should voluntarily submit themselves to examination in order to lower their borrowing costs. Annual Article IV consultations could be supplemented by quarterly reviews that would enhance the credibility of the data released under the IMF's recent initiative and thus help to reduce the costs of adjustment programs.

References

Calvo, Guillermo A., "Capital Flows and Macroeconomic Management: Tequila Lessons," University of Maryland, Department of Economics, December 1995, processed.

Calvo, Guillermo A., Leonardo Leiderman, and Carmen M. Reinhart, "Capital Inflows and Real Exchange Rate Appreciation in Latin America," *International Monetary Fund Staff Papers*, 40 (March 1993), pp. 108–151.

Dornbusch, Rudiger, and Alejandro Werner, "Mexico: Stabilization, Reform and No Growth," *Brookings Papers on Economic Activity*, 1 (1994), pp. 253–297.

Fraga, Arminio, *German Reparations and Brazilian Debt: A Comparative Study*, Essays in International Finance No. 163, Princeton, N.J., Princeton University, International Finance Section, July 1986.

Institute of International Finance (IIF), *Mexico Country Report*, Washington, D.C., Institute of International Finance, May 13, 1996.

International Monetary Fund (IMF), *World Economic Outlook*, Washington, D.C., International Monetary Fund, May 1995a.

————, *International Capital Markets: Developments, Prospects and Policy Issues*, Washington, D.C., International Monetary Fund, August 1995b.

Leiderman, Leonardo, and Alfredo Thorne, "The 1994 Mexican Crisis and Its Aftermath: What Are the Main Lessons," in Guillermo Calvo, Morris Goldstein, and Eduard Hochreiter, eds., *Private Capital Flows to Emerging Markets After the Mexican Crisis*, Washington, D.C., Institute for International Economics, 1996, pp. 1–43.

AVOIDING FUTURE MEXICOS: A POST-HALIFAX SCORECARD ON CRISIS PREVENTION AND MANAGEMENT

Morris Goldstein

There is nothing like a crisis to motivate a review of crisis prevention and management. The proposals launched at the Group of Seven (G–7) Economic Summit in Halifax in June 1995 and pursued at the interim committee meetings of the International Monetary Fund (IMF) in October 1995 and April 1996 and at the Group of Seven (G–7) Summit in Lyons in June 1996 reflect the official sector's interpretation of the lessons learned from the Mexican crisis.

My appraisal of what has been accomplished since Halifax, as well as of what still needs to be done, concentrates on four areas: (1) vulnerabilities and policies in emerging-market economies, (2) data disclosure and market discipline, (3) the speed and size of international lender-of-last-resort facilities, and (4) orderly workouts for sovereign-bond defaults.

1 Vulnerabilities and Policies of Debtor Countries

The first line of defense against financial crises in debtor countries must be macroeconomic, prudential, and structural policies that reduce the vulnerability of these countries to currency, banking, and debt crises. The burgeoning literature on the determinants of financial crises in emerging markets suggests that these vulnerabilities encompass both flow and stock measures of disequilibria and external as well as internal sources of trouble (Frankel and Rose, 1995; Goldstein, 1996a; Kaminsky and Reinhart, 1996; Sachs, Tornell, and Velasco, 1996).

A good summary of the sources of vulnerability is provided by what I call the seven deadly sins (Goldstein, 1996a); these are (1) an upward turn in international interest rates, (2) a growing mismatch between the government's liquid, short-term liabilities, the banking system's liquid, short-term liabilities, or both, and the stock of international reserves, (3) a large current-account deficit, used mainly to increase consumption and financed in good measure by short-term and foreign-denominated

I am indebted to C. Fred Bergsten, Geoffrey Carliner, and John Williamson for comments on an earlier draft.

borrowing, (4) a highly overvalued real exchange rate, exacerbated by the "politicization" of exchange-rate policy decisions, (5) severe constraints (related to financial fragility or high unemployment) on the willingness to increase domestic interest rates in the face of a significant falloff in private-capital inflows, (6) a boom in bank lending, coupled with a sharp fall in equity prices, real estate prices, or both, and (7) relatively high vulnerability to "contagion" from financial disturbances originating elsewhere (with this vulnerability reflecting, *inter alia*, regional effects, small size, and a poor policy track record that encourages a "flight to quality").

Three policy measures in host countries would be most effective in reducing these vulnerabilities. First, banking systems in emerging markets must be made more resilient to large and abrupt shifts in the flows of private capital, and the quality of banking supervision must be substantially upgraded. When the domestic banking system is already under strain, monetary authorities in host countries will be severely constrained in their conduct of interest-rate policy for fear of pushing banks over the edge. Such a constraint, however, will remove from the defending central bank's arsenal one of the main policy instruments it has for dealing with volatile private-capital flows, especially during a currency crisis. Between 1991 and mid-1994, the share of nonperforming loans doubled in Mexico's banks. This banking-sector weakness probably explains better than anything else why the Mexican authorities (from April through December 1994) both sterilized so heavily after private-capital flows tailed off and engaged in large-scale substitution of lower-yielding dollar-indexed tesobonos for higher-yielding, peso-denominated cetes. Both actions were aimed at limiting the rise in interest rates and buying time for the banks to recover. In the end, however, these measures fueled the size and speed of the fall in international reserves, allowed a currency crisis to widen into a debt crisis, and limited the role that exchange-rate depreciation could play in getting out of the crisis (Calvo and Goldstein, 1996; Sachs, Tornell, and Velasco, 1995). It may be recalled that Sweden's inability to sustain very high interest rates during the 1992 exchange-rate mechanism (ERM) crisis reflected similar difficulties.

More important than the adverse effect of weak banking systems on currency-crisis defenses is the potential in emerging markets for these weak systems to develop into full-blown financial crises of their own. The experiences of the 1980s and 1990s amply demonstrate this possibility. The list of current and recent casualties includes, among others, Brazil, Bulgaria, Hungary, Indonesia, Mexico, Poland, Romania, Venezuela, and

Zimbabwe. Aside from the frequency of banking crises, what is striking about them is the magnitude of the resolution costs. Current estimates, for example, put the accumulated losses in the recent Bulgarian, Hungarian, Mexican, and Venezuelan banking crises in the neighborhood of 10 to 20 percent of their respective GDPs; the Argentinean and Chilean banking crises of the earlier 1980s were even more costly (Caprio and Klingebiel, 1996). One recent study (Honohan, 1996) estimates that resolution costs of banking crises in all developing and transitional economies since 1990 are close to $250 billion.[1] When faced with costs of this magnitude, it becomes much more difficult to control fiscal deficits, avoid credit crunches for small and medium-sized floats, and obtain the productive investment so crucial to good growth performance (Lindgren, Garcia, and Saal, 1996).

Too often, the ingredients for a banking crisis are all present: low bank capital relative to the high volatility of the operating environment (for example, large terms-of-trade shocks, a high incidence of serious recessions, high real-exchange-rate volatility associated with sharp fluctuations in inflation rates, and sharp swings in private capital flows); efforts by governments to use the banking system to prop up ailing industries, or to help fund government deficits (and to conceal that funding by doing it off-budget) or both; too-liberal access to banking licenses, along with high shares of connected lending; asset-classification rules that delay the identification of nonperforming loans and lend themselves to the "evergreening" of bad assets; heavy political pressures for regulatory forbearance when corrective action, or the closure of banks, or both, should be the preferred course of action; reluctance to expand the resources devoted to banking supervision prior to capital-market liberalization; occasional heavy reliance on short-term foreign-currency-denominated liabilities in the wholesale interbank market to fund domestic long-term lending; exchange-rate regimes that limit severely the latitude of the central bank to act as lender of last resort during a bank run; absence of adequately funded deposit insurance for small investors; a track record of large-scale bailouts for uninsured creditors in earlier banking crises; and poor accounting systems in general, along with lack of public information on the creditworthiness of individual banks (Folkerts-Landau et al., 1995; Rojas-Suarez and Weisbrod, 1995, Goldstein and Turner, 1996).

The ultimate question is how to strengthen banking systems and banking supervision in emerging markets—and how to do it quickly.

---

[1] Here and throughout, billion equals a thousand million.

Clearly, the current case-by-case strategy, supported by the existing international accords and concordats, is not getting the job done. Having IMF surveillance devote greater attention to financial and banking-sector developments is not likely by itself to overcome the problem, helpful though such increased attention would be. Given the political resistance to reform, the answer is also apt to lie beyond extending more technical assistance to emerging markets, although such assistance would surely be useful. For the time being, market discipline will be constrained by the paucity of publicly available information on the creditworthiness of borrowers and by the expectation of public-sector bailouts of troubled borrowers. Relying on banking crises in individual countries to provide the motivation for reform is hardly attractive either, given the costs involved. What is needed is a major international effort.

Because banking problems are both severe and common in many developing countries, the time is ripe for an international banking standard (IBS).[2] Such a standard should be jointly sponsored by the international financial institutions (the IMF, the Bank for International Settlements [BIS], the World Bank, and the regional development banks), in consultation with the Basle Committee, representatives of the banking industry, and the supervisory and regulatory authorities in developing countries. Subscription to the standard should be voluntary, and there should be a reasonable transition period to give countries time to adapt their practices. Once a country subscribes to the standard, adherence to it—or progress toward it—could be monitored by the country missions of the international financial institutions (admittedly, this would require these institutions to deepen their expertise on banking supervision, along with national banking supervisors). The list of countries meeting the international banking standard should be made public. The standard should be regarded as a minimum, and national governments might choose to set higher standards in their own legislation and practices.

The elements of an IBS should be limited in number and directed toward those banking and supervisory practices most in need of reform.

---

[2] I do not regard the recommendations issued by the Basle Committee as constituting an IBS. Existing international banking agreements do not address many of the factors generating banking fragility in developing countries. Nor do they take account of the special circumstances of developing countries in defining risk-based capital requirements (Goldstein 1996b). In addition, these agreements are not monitored by an international agency, and the countries adhering or not adhering to the agreement are not publicly identified on a regular basis.

The following seven reforms should receive priority.[3] (1) *Disclosure*: Participants should be required to publish basic information on bank performance, bank income, and bank balance sheets, prepared in accordance with international accounting standards; (2) *Accounting and legal framework*: Participants would agree to institute loan-classification practices that give appropriate weight (*inter alia*) to a current assessment of the borrower's repayment capacity (not just to the loan's current payment status), to place an agreed upon limit on the length of time a loan may be in arrears before it is classified as nonperforming, and to review their respective legal codes and to certify that bank supervisors have the statutory authority to carry out their mandate; (3) *Government involvement*: Participants would agree to include quasi-fiscal operations of governments vis-á-vis the banking system in central-government budget statements, as well as to publish on a regular basis data on the loan-loss experience of state-owned banks; (4) *Connected lending*: Participants would agree to establish exposure limits on lending to connected parties, to disclose publicly the share of loans made to connected parties, and to outlaw practices that make it difficult or impossible for supervisors to verify the accuracy of reported connected-lending exposure; (5) *Bank capital*: Participants would agree to apply an agreed upon "safety factor" to the existing Basle risk-weighted standard if their recent history of loan defaults, restructured loans, and government assistance to troubled banks has been significantly higher than the OECD average over, say, the past five years; (6) *Political pressures on bank supervisors*: Participants would agree to institute certain "prompt corrective-action" procedures when bank capital drops below pre-specified zones—along the lines of the provisions contained in the U.S. Federal Deposit Insurance Corporation Improvement Act of 1991; and (7) *Consolidated supervision*. Participants would agree to implement the 1992 Basle minimum standards on globally consolidated supervision and on cooperation among host and home-country banking supervisors.

A cue might be taken from the Basle risk-weighted capital standards, from the Group of Thirty best-practice guidelines on derivatives, and from the IMF's recently agreed upon special data dissemination standard (SDDS). In each case, it was decided that international standards or guidelines offered incentives for countries and firms to make improvements in either the financial infrastructure or their own risk-

---

[3] See Goldstein (1996b) for a more complete exposition of the elements of an IBS and for a discussion of the way in which the requirements for participation in the base (interim) standard ought to differ from those for the stricter, high-level standard.

management systems that they might not have been able or willing to make acting alone, because of entrenched opposition at home or domestic and international competitiveness. Even when adherence to the standard is voluntary, knowledge by market participants of who is and is not meeting the standard tends to establish market penalties for slow movers.[4] Those countries whose national practices already exceed the minimum international standard would not be constrained by it and would receive some assurance that the creditworthiness of their counterparts had improved.

A second policy area with considerable scope for improvement is exchange-rate policy, along with holdings of international reserves. It should be clear from both the ERM and Mexican crises that attempting to hold onto a significantly overvalued, publicly announced exchange-rate target is risky business, even if it is tempting on political grounds for incumbents to delay devaluation until after an election.

This does not mean that countries with poor records on inflation and no preferential alternative to the exchange rate as a nominal anchor should eschew exchange-rate-based stabilization. It does suggest, however, that a way needs to be found to exit from a rigid exchange-rate commitment to more exchange-rate flexibility before the common tendency to marked appreciation in the real exchange rate reaches the point at which its sustainability becomes suspect. In this connection, Hausman and Gavin (1995) find that unsustainable exchange-rate pegs have contributed more to the relatively high volatility of economic growth in Latin American than has any other factor. Managed floating, along with domestic inflation targets, crawling exchange-rate bands (as in Chile, Colombia, and Israel), and a simple widening of the bands during periods of pressure from capital markets all merit consideration.[5] Relative to fixed rates (along with narrow margins), these more flexible arrangements should serve to moderate surges of capital

---

[4] In addition to market incentives for meeting the standard, consideration could also be given to, for example, adjusting the risk weights (for credit risk) in the Basle capital standards to reflect compliance with the IBS. This would be preferable to the current practice of giving a risk weight of zero to obligations of industrial countries subscribing to the General Arrangements to Borrow (GAB) and a risk weight of 100 percent to those of all other countries. Similarly, the terms and conditions of access to international lender-of-last resort facilities could be made contingent on, among other factors, the borrowing country's adoption of the IBS; this would increase the payoff to taking crisis-prevention measures.

[5] These attractions of exchange-rate flexibility seem to be increasingly recognized. Whereas in 1975, fewer than one-fifth of all IMF member countries adhered to flexible

inflows and to conserve on reserves when capital flows reverse direction. In addition, leaving more of the initiative for changes in the exchange rate to market forces or predetermined formulas will make exchange rates less susceptible to misalignments stemming from the "politicization" of exchange-rate policy decisions.

Even when the choice is for a fixed-rate, discretionary exchange-rate regime, the internal political pressures for delay of needed readjustments can be offset in part by countervailing peer pressure from multilateral and bilateral official sources. In this respect, the G–7's call for franker advice from the IMF is right on target. As I have argued elsewhere (Goldstein, 1995), the IMF has to be prepared (confidentially, at first) to press hard for prompt correction of a highly overvalued exchange rate, even when the home country has not asked for that advice, and the IMF's shareholders have to be prepared to hold the Fund accountable for relaying that message at a time when it counts.

Reserve management also has a role to play in crisis prevention. The tequila effect of the Mexican crisis illustrates that, at least in the short term, the contagion of financial disturbances can go beyond what would be implied by the fundamentals (IMF, 1995; Calvo and Reinhart, 1996; Valdes, 1996). Recent empirical studies suggest that vulnerability to currency and banking crises in emerging markets has in the past been inversely related to a country's holding of international reserves (Calvo and Goldstein, 1996; Sachs, Tornell, and Velasco, 1996). Assessing reserve adequacy with respect to imports alone no longer makes much sense for countries heavily involved with private-capital markets. If net reserves are intended to capture proximity to a balance-of-payments crisis, then all short-term obligations of the government (explicit and implicit) should be considered as candidates for subtraction from gross reserves. In short, with large and volatile international capital markets, a healthy reserve cushion has taken on increased importance. On this score, the recent "repo" agreement among a group of Asian countries to establish mutual lines of assistance based on holdings of U.S. Treasury securities in their reserves is a positive development.

A third route to decreased host-country vulnerability is prudent management of government debt. This means keeping a tight lid on short-term debt and on debt denominated in foreign currencies. The temptation to do otherwise is the interest-rate saving that results from

arrangements of one type or another, by 1993, that share had risen to one-half (Eichengreen, 1994). For a recent analysis of country experience with crawling exchange-rate bands, see Williamson (1996).

having the borrower assume currency risk and rollover risk. Some writers have also stressed the "precommitment advantages" of foreign-currency borrowing. As the Mexican experience vividly illustrates, however, such a borrowing policy by the government can easily have long-term costs that swamp any short-term saving. Dooley (1995) argues convincingly that in a world in which currency and rollover risk can be influenced strongly by events beyond the borrower's control (for example, changes in international interest rates), emerging-market borrowers have a more spotted record on default than do industrial countries, and constraints elsewhere in the financial system limit the scope for an aggressive interest defense of the currency; borrowers have to worry about the variance of borrowing costs—not just average cost. Moreover, foreign-currency borrowing not only increases the chances of getting into a crisis, it also makes it harder to get out of one, because it renders the traditional remedy—easier monetary policy, or devaluation, or both—much less effective (Mishkin, 1996). Although developing countries just reentering the capital market may therefore have little choice but to accept very short maturities and foreign-currency denomination to get their "toes in the water," those that are more established should manage their debt conservatively with respect to currency and rollover risk.

2 Data Disclosure and Private-Market Discipline

Private-capital markets will not be able to price risk appropriately or to discipline errant borrowers unless market participants have timely and comprehensive information on the borrower's creditworthiness. According to the Group of Thirty (1995), published data on Mexico's international reserves (in 1994) reached the market late—sometimes as much as six months late. More broadly, a recent report by the Institute of International Finance (IIF, 1996) documents that emerging markets differ quite significantly in their current practices toward the publication of basic economic and financial data. The Czech Republic, Israel, Mexico, Peru, the Philippines, and South Korea, for example, each met the IIF standards on both periodicity and timeliness for at least 15 of the 18 data series considered, whereas the corresponding scores for China, Greece, India, Morocco, Russia, and South Africa were 5 or less.

Seen in this light, the SDDS recently agreed upon by the IMF's interim committee for countries involved in international capital markets is a definite step forward. The aspects of disclosure addressed by the standard (coverage, periodicity, timeliness, public access, and quality and integrity of the data) touch all the important points, and the plan to have the IMF operate an electronic bulletin board (that would list the countries subscribing to the standard, along with relevant information about country data) is a good one. Two caveats nevertheless merit explicit mention.

First, because participation in the SDDS is voluntary, incentives to comply with it depend in good measure on market participants knowing which countries are in good standing and which countries are not. Although the SDDS calls for the IMF to take a country "off the board" if it ceases to observe the standard (after the completion of the transition period), such removal is the last stage in a set of graduated measures. If the intervening stages are prolonged, any market penalties for delay or manipulation will be much reduced. It would have been better for the Fund to have set a specific time limit for handling country appeals before reporting noncompliance to the market.

Second, as crucial as good information is to the functioning of financial markets, it is by no means the only cause of financial crises. Indeed, a review of several recent episodes of market turbulence reveals that the major initiating factor behind abrupt shifts in private-capital flows was not inadequate information but, rather, faulty economic analysis accompanied by unexpected developments. A good example is the ERM crisis. The $300 billion or so that flowed into the high-interest-rate ERM currencies from 1987 to 1992 (so-called "convergence plays") reflected the assumption that the sizable interest differential over deutsche mark assets was less and less a premium for bearing currency risk. The unexpected outcome of the Danish referendum led markets to rethink their views about currency risk and the inevitability of EMU, and the rush to the exits followed (Goldstein et al., 1993). This surely will not be the last time market participants take large (often highly leveraged) bets on the future course of interest and exchange rates and get it wrong. For this reason, I have suggested that the IMF ought to share more of its views on policy fundamentals and exchange rates with the private markets by publishing its Article IV country reports (Goldstein, 1995). In a similar vein, even when markets have complete information, market discipline will not operate well if a public bailout of the borrower is expected. In that case, the interest rate will reflect the creditworthiness of the guarantor, not that of the borrower. One explanation why the measured default premium on tesobonos never rose above 3 percent in the six months just before the Mexican crisis is that Mexico was seen as too large and too important to the United States to be allowed to fail. In the end, the more than

$50 billion in official support did allow holders of tesobonos to get out whole. Efforts to decrease the expectation of future public bailouts are discussed below.

3 The Speed and Size of International Lender-of-Last-Resort Facilities

Judging from their subsequent recommendations, G–7 crisis managers apparently drew the conclusion from their experience in the Mexican crisis that the speed and size of existing international lender-of-last resort facilities were inadequate. They therefore created the emergency-financing mechanism (EFM) to increase the speed of official response and proposed a doubling of the GAB (from roughly $25 billion to $50 billion) to permit larger official financial support.

There are two main constraints on the speed of emergency financial assistance. One is the need to review the borrowing country's economic situation and to negotiate the policy conditionality for such assistance. Policy conditionality not only serves as the commitment technology to overcome potential time-inconsistency problems and as a means to generate the foreign exchange that will be used to repay official creditors on time, it can also be seen as the costly "coinsurance" premium that reduces moral hazard. Even in crisis situations, such a review, along with negotiation, would normally be expected to take a few weeks. This process could be accelerated by preapproving the borrower for the loan at, say, the time of the most recent Article IV consultation by the IMF. Because such preapproval would both increase the risk of default (the borrower's creditworthiness could change markedly between the time of preapproval and the timing of the drawing) and increase moral hazard, it has quite rightly been rejected. The EFM, which despite its more lofty name deals with mundane procedural matters, is not likely to loosen this time constraint.

The second source of delay (once the borrowing country and the IMF staff and management have agreed) is the need to get the approval of the IMF's executive board. The board members also need to be convinced that the policy conditions and scale of assistance are appropriate. Recall that several European countries abstained on the IMF loan to Mexico, in part because they thought they were not consulted adequately (they may also have thought that the consequences of a Mexican default would be more regional than systemic, and that a loan for an extraordinary 700 percent of quota was therefore ill advised). The U.S. Treasury and the IMF management responded that the urgency of the situation precluded more extensive consultation. This is an example of a case in which the newly established EFM should help. The EFM will compress the period for reviewing the loan documents, brief the Fund's executive directors on the crisis early on, and, by giving the Fund's directors a large role in the negotiations, will reduce the frequency of contacts with national capitals. This is sensible housekeeping that reflects the procedural lessons learned from the Mexican case.

The proposal to double the size of the GAB might be defended on at least three grounds. First, the size of international reserves, IMF quotas, and supplemental lines of credit, such as the GAB, need to increase in tandem with the secular growth of world trade and payments. Second, the increased integration of national capital markets decreases the likelihood that a significant financial disturbance will remain localized (see Goldstein and Mussa, 1994, and Cashin, Kumar, and McDermott, 1995, on increasing integration). Such spillover effects not only increase the potential size of demands for emergency financial assistance, they also create confusion about which national central bank or treasury will have responsibility for extending lender-of-last resort assistance.[6] Third, the political difficulties of trying to have one national government impose policy conditionality on another, along with fiscal pressures and considerations of burden sharing in the major creditor countries, argue for responding to cross-border market failures through an international, rather than national, lender of last resort (Calvo and Goldstein, 1996; Rodrik, 1995).

The main concern with expanding the GAB is that such expansion might be perceived as decreasing the incentives of private lenders to monitor the creditworthiness of the borrower, because larger official resources are potentially available in the case of an impending default or currency depreciation. The official sector has tried to minimize such moral hazard by stipulating that an expanded GAB would remain subject to strict policy conditionality and that access to it would continue to be restricted to systemic threats. The credibility of its claim that the GAB will not in the future be easily available in amounts such as those given Mexico is bolstered by two facts: the GAB has not been activated since the late 1970s, and the $50 billion-plus rescue package for Mexico (financed outside the GAB) was so difficult to put together that future mega-rescue packages look increasingly unsalable (see Kenen, 1996, for

[6] Masson and Mussa (1995) show that roughly one-third of forty-nine industrial and middle-income developing countries suffered a maximum, monthly reserve loss equal to 100 percent or more of their IMF quotas during the period from 1985 to 1993.

a brief history of the GAB). In this latter connection, recall that the U.S. Congress rejected the Clinton administration's original request for a $40 billion loan guarantee for Mexico, and that there would likely be strong congressional opposition to again using the Treasury's Exchange Stabilization Fund for a loan on the order of (Mexico's) $20 billion. Most important, the official sector seems to have emerged from its eighteen months of reflection since the outbreak of the Mexican crisis with a definite "tilt" toward suspension and restructuring of sovereign-bond debt and away from large-scale financing to avoid it (see below). Giving the official sector an enhanced capability to intervene forcefully to aid a solvent but illiquid borrower when a systemic threat exists is not, therefore, the same as concluding that this capability will surely be used more frequently than in the past.

4 Orderly Workouts for Sovereign-Bond Defaults

Like Wagner's music, the G–10 report (1996) on the resolution of sovereign-liquidity crises is better than it sounds. Recall that at the outbreak of the Mexican crisis in December 1994, no one knew (including, I think, the official sector itself) what official attitudes were on the restructuring of sovereign bonds. There was a Paris Club for the restructuring of official debt and a London Club for the restructuring of commercial bank debt, but there was nothing for sovereign bonds. When the crisis came, official creditors faced two unpalatable options: to allow Mexico to default on tesobonos and accept a potentially very deep recession in Mexico (as private capital dried up), along with an unknown degree of contagion to other emerging markets or, alternatively, to provide unprecedented official assistance in support of Mexico's adjustment effort and to accept the moral-hazard precedent inherent in such intervention, along with some risk of nonrepayment. In consideration of Mexico's informal "benchmark" status among emerging-market borrowers as well as the particularly large adverse spillover effects (political and economic) of a Mexican default for the United States, the choice was for the latter option. It was, in the words of Federal Reserve Chairman Greenspan (1995), the "least worst" of the alternatives available.

The G–10 report attempts to carve out a "third option" that would relieve G–10 creditors of some of the cost of financial crisis, by shifting more of the burden to both private creditors and debtor countries. In addition, the report seeks to reduce future uncertainty by clarifying the "rules of the game" for sovereign-liquidity crises. Of the conclusions and principles endorsed by the report, two merit particular attention.

First, a key recommendation is to have the IMF review its financing-assurances policy so that it can lend to a debtor that is in arrears to private creditors—not just on bank loans but also on sovereign bonds. This would allow the IMF to provide the "debtor-in-possession" financing that is needed during debt workouts. Even though this policy would stop short of an official endorsement of a payments standstill, it should decrease the leverage that private creditors have on debtors to meet their contractual obligations in exceptionally adverse circumstances. So long as the debtor is making a strong adjustment effort and making reasonable efforts to negotiate with creditors, the country can qualify for support from the official sector. This would make it more difficult for private creditors to win a war of attrition. The influence of G–7 creditors in this respect should not be underestimated. The shift from Baker to Brady, along with the Fund's decision to lend into arrears on private bank debt, were essential elements in accelerating the resolution of the 1980s debt crisis.

The report also puts teeth behind the principle that orderly workout procedures should "strengthen the ability of governments to resist pressures to assume responsibility for the external liabilities of their private sectors." It softens its recommendations by urging that procedures be "cooperative and nonconfrontational," and by reaffirming the principle that "the terms and conditions of all debt contracts should be met in full." But make no mistake, the report does tilt toward debtors. In the end, moral hazard cannot be reduced without allowing private lenders to suffer some of the costs of poor lending decisions, costs for which they receive compensation *ex ante* by the significant currency and default premia on emerging-market debt. This is a desirable shift in attitude on the part of the official sector, decreasing the probability that official safety nets will be overused in the future; by clarifying official policy and reducing the cost of payments suspension to debtors, it makes the alternative to withholding official support easier to accept.

Second, the report quite sensibly concludes that a formal international bankruptcy code would not be feasible, either now or in the foreseeable future, because the practical obstacles are simply too formidable (Eichengreen and Portes, 1995; Calvo and Goldstein, 1996). It instead encourages sovereign borrowers and their creditors to work out their own contractual arrangements with a view toward providing collective representation of debt holders (for example, bondholders' councils), allowing qualified majority voting to alter the terms and conditions of debt contracts, and extending the sharing clause to sovereign-bond contracts. The form of official support for such efforts is left unstated; it will be provided "as appropriate."

The question is whether this ambiguity will act as an impediment to the implementation of such contractual changes. Emerging-market debtors, for example, will be more inclined to introduce a clause for qualified majority voting in their bond issues if such a clause can be seen as serving the recontracting interest of both debtors and creditors, rather than as signaling a weakening of the debtor's commitment to the original contract; if it is seen as the latter, creditors will demand a risk premium for its introduction. It will be hard to exclude such a signal, however, if bonds of only the least creditworthy borrowers contain such a clause. By not agreeing to include this provision in their own future bond issues, the G–10 makes it less likely that such a contractual innovation will be "market led." Similarly, private creditors may only be willing to endorse qualified majority voting if dissident creditors have access to a binding tribunal. If no one knows beforehand whether such a tribunal will be supported by the official sector, however, majority-voting clauses may not get off the ground. A parallel argument can be made for the creation of bondholders' councils. If the official sector believes that changes in bond contracts will be in the public interest, it should be prepared to be more transparent in its support for such changes.

5 Conclusion

To sum up, I give the G–7, the G–10, and the IMF good marks on an international data standard, on upgrading the capability of the international lender of last resort, and on setting out a policy line for orderly workouts that shifts more of the cost for resolving sovereign-liquidity crises back to private creditors and debtor countries. Before the Lyons Summit, I would have given them failing marks for being too slow and too timid in moving forward on what is likely to be the dominant source of future financial crises in emerging markets, namely, weak banking systems and weak banking supervision. Based on the language in the Lyons Communiqué, however, it now looks as though the G–7 is prepared to pledge its support for some sort of international banking standard or guidelines. This is a welcome conversion. The next year will tell whether or not the proposed standard has real teeth.

References

Calvo, Guillermo, and Morris Goldstein, "Crisis Prevention and Crisis Management After Mexico: What Role for the Official Sector?" in Guillermo

Calvo, Morris Goldstein, and Eduard Hochreiter, eds., *Private Capital Flows to Emerging Markets After the Mexican Crisis*, Washington, D.C., Institute for International Economics, 1996, pp. 233–282.

Calvo, Sara, and Carmen Reinhart, "Capital Flows to Latin America: Is There Evidence of 'Contagion' Effects?" in Guillermo Calvo, Morris Goldstein, and Eduard Hochreiter, eds., *Private Capital Flows to Emerging Markets After the Mexican Crisis*, Washington, D.C., Institute for International Economics, 1996, pp. 151–171.

Caprio, Gerald, and Daniela Klingebiel, "Bank Insolvency: Bad Luck, Bad Policy, or Bad Banking?" paper presented at World Bank Conference on Development Economics, Washington, D.C., April 25–26, 1996.

Cashin, Paul, Manmohan Kumar, and C. John McDermott, "International Integration of Equity Markets and Contagion Effects," International Monetary Fund Working Paper No. 95/110, Washington, International Monetary Fund, November 1995.

Dooley, Michael, "Managing the Public Debt," paper presented at the World Bank conference on Managing Economic Reform under Capital Flow Volatility, Washington, D.C., May 30–June 2, 1995.

Eichengreen, Barry, *International Monetary Arrangements for the Twenty-First Century*, Washington, D.C., Brookings Institution, 1994.

Eichengreen, Barry, and Richard Portes, *Crisis? What Crisis? Orderly Workouts for Sovereign Debtors*, London, Centre for Economic Policy Research, 1995.

Folkerts-Landau, David, Garry Schinasi, Marcel Cassard, Victor Ng, Carmen Reinhart, and Michael Spencer, "Effects of Capital Flows on the Domestic Financial Sectors in APEC Developing Countries," in Mohsin Khan and Carmen Reinhart, eds., *Capital Flows in the APEC Region*, Occasional Paper 122, Washington, D.C., International Monetary Fund, March 1995.

Frankel, Jeffrey, and Andrew Rose, "Exchange Rate Crashes in Emerging Markets: An Empirical Treatment," University of California at Berkeley, Department of Economics, November 1995, processed.

Goldstein, Morris, *Have Flexible Exchange Rates Handicapped Macroeconomic Policy?* Special Papers in International Economics No. 14, Princeton, N.J., Princeton University, International Finance Section, June 1980.

——, *The Exchange Rate System and the IMF: A Modest Agenda*, Policy Analyses in International Economics No. 39, Washington, D.C., Institute for International Economics, June 1995.

——, "Presumptive Indicators/Early Warning Signals of Vulnerability to Financial Crises in Emerging-Market Economies," Washington, D.C., Institute for International Economics, January 1996a, processed.

——, "The Case for an International Banking Standard," Washington, D.C., Institute for International Economics, August 1996b, processed.

Goldstein, Morris, David Folkerts-Landau, Peter Garber, Liliana Rojas-Suarez, and Michael Spencer, *International Capital Markets Report: Exchange Rate Management and International Capital Flows*, World Economic and Finan-

70

cial Surveys, Washington, D.C., International Monetary Fund, April 1993.

Goldstein, Morris, and Michael Mussa, "The Integration of World Capital Markets," in *Changing Capital Markets*, Kansas City, Mo., Federal Reserve Bank of Kansas City, 1994, pp. 245–314.

Goldstein, Morris, and Philip Turner, *Banking Crises in Emerging Economies: Origins and Policy Options*, BIS Economic Papers No. 46, Basle, Bank for International Settlements, October 1996.

Group of Ten (G–10), *The Resolution of Sovereign Liquidity Crises: A Report to the Ministers and Governors*, Basle, Bank for International Settlements, and Washington, D.C., International Monetary Fund, May 1996.

Hausman, Ricardo, and Michael Gavin, "Macroeconomic Volatility in Latin America: Causes, Consequences, and Policies to Assure Stability," Washington, D.C., Inter-American Development Bank, July 1995, processed.

Honohan, Patrick, "Financial System Failures in Developing Countries: Diagnosis and Prescriptions," Washington, D.C., International Monetary Fund, June 1996.

Institute of International Finance, *Data Release Standards for Emerging Economies: An Assessment of Country Practices*, Washington, D.C., Institute of International Finance, April 1996.

International Monetary Fund (IMF), *International Capital Markets Report*, World Economic and Financial Surveys, Washington, D.C., International Monetary Fund, August 1995.

Kaminsky, Graciela, and Carmen Reinhart, "The Twin Crises: The Causes of Banking and Balance of Payments Problems," International Finance Discussion Paper No. 544, Washington, D.C., Board of Governors of the Federal Reserve, March 1996.

Kenen, Peter, "Analyzing and Managing Exchange Rate Crises," Princeton University, Department of Economics, May 1996, processed.

Lindgren, Carl-Johan, Gillian Garcia, and Matthew Saal, *Bank Soundness and Macroeconomic Policy*, Washington, D.C., International Monetary Fund, September 1996

Masson, Paul, and Michael Mussa, "The Role of the Fund: Financing and its Interaction with Adjustment and Surveillance," Washington, D.C., International Monetary Fund, 1995, processed.

Mishkin, Frederic, "Asymmetric Information and Financial Crises: A Developing Country Perspective," New York, Federal Reserve Bank of New York, March 1996, processed.

Rodrik, Dani, "Why Is There Multilateral Lending?" CEPR Discussion Paper No. 1207, London, Centre for Economic Policy Research, July 1995.

Rojas-Suarez, Liliana, and Steven Weisbrod, *Financial Fragilities in Latin America: The 1980s and 1990s*, Occasional Paper No. 132, Washington, D.C., International Monetary Fund, October 1995.

Sachs, Jeffrey, Aaron Tornell, and Andrés Velasco, "The Collapse of the Mexican Peso: What Have We Learned?" Harvard University, Department of Economics, May 1995, processed.

71

———, "Financial Crises in Emerging Markets: The Lessons from 1995," Harvard University, Department of Economics, March 1996, processed.

Valdes, Rodrigo, "Emerging Markets Contagion: Evidence and Theory," Massachusetts Institute of Technology, Department of Economics, February 1996, processed.

Williamson, John, *The Crawling Band as an Exchange Rate Regime*, Washington, D.C., Institute for International Economics, September 1996.

GROUP OF TEN

THE RESOLUTION OF SOVEREIGN LIQUIDITY CRISES

A report to the Ministers and Governors
prepared under the auspices of the Deputies

Pre-publication version

May 1996

EXECUTIVE SUMMARY

1. Following an invitation to the Ministers and Governors of the Group of Ten by the Heads of State and Government of the Group of Seven in Halifax in June 1995, the Deputies of the Group of Ten established a working party to consider the complex set of issues arising with respect to the orderly resolution of sovereign liquidity crises. While taking a comprehensive view of the problem, the Working Party focused its attention on those forms of debt to private creditors, such as internationally traded securities, that have increased in importance in the new financial environment but that in the past have usually been shielded from payments suspensions or restructurings. In carrying out its work, the Working Party recognised that the highest priority needs to be given to measures that will help prevent crises from occurring and endorsed efforts underway in other forums to improve market discipline and strengthen the surveillance of sovereign borrowers' economic performance. It attached particular importance to the need for sovereign borrowers to make timely changes in their economic policies if conditions change in ways that may lead to reductions in capital inflows.

2. After careful review of analyses of the full range of questions involved, and taking into consideration surveys of the views of market participants and of legal practices relating to collective representation of debt holders that were conducted by its members for this purpose, the Working Party reached the following broad conclusions.
- First, it is essential to maintain the basic principles that the terms and conditions of all debt contracts are to be met in full and that market discipline must be preserved. However, in exceptional cases, a temporary suspension of debt payments by the debtor may be unavoidable as part of the

73

process of crisis resolution and as a way of gaining time to put in place a credible adjustment programme.

- Second, neither debtor countries nor their creditors should expect to be insulated from adverse financial consequences by the provision of large-scale official financing in the event of a crisis. Markets are equipped, or should be equipped, to assess the risks involved in lending to sovereign borrowers and to set the prices and other terms of the instruments accordingly. There should be no presumption that any type of debt will be exempt from payments suspensions or restructurings in the event of a future sovereign liquidity crisis.

- Third, current flexible, case-by-case practices and procedures, as they have evolved over the years, are an appropriate starting point for approaches to sovereign liquidity crises. They emphasise the importance of adjustment efforts of the debtor country and place principal responsibility for workouts on the debtors and creditors, with the debtor country having primary responsibility for setting the process on a co-operative footing. Improvements in practices and procedures should continue to be evolutionary.

- Fourth, international bankruptcy procedures and other formal arrangements do not appear to provide, in current circumstances or in the foreseeable future, a feasible or appropriate way of dealing with sovereign liquidity crises. However, further study by private sector entities may be warranted.

- Fifth, further consideration should be given in appropriate forums to ways in which financial systems in emerging market economies could be strengthened in order to reduce the risks they might pose in the event of a sovereign liquidity crisis.

- Sixth, a market-led process to develop for inclusion in sovereign debt instruments contractual provisions that facilitate consultation and cooperation between debtors and their private creditors, as well as within the creditor community, in the event of crisis would be desirable. Market initiatives would deserve official support as appropriate.

- And seventh, note was taken of current policies of the IMF that provide, under exceptional circumstances, for lending in support of effective adjustment programmes prior to full and final resolution of a sovereign borrower's arrears to private creditors. It would be advisable for the IMF Executive Board to review existing policy in this area and to consider whether the scope of its application should be extended to other forms of debt not now covered, while remaining mindful of the need for prudence and the maintenance of strict conditionality.

3. The thinking of the Working Party was influenced by three basic changes in the financial environment bearing on the character of potential future sovereign liquidity crises. First, the broader and stronger linkages among domestic and international financial markets mean that crises can erupt much more quickly in today's markets and can be far larger in scope than in the past. Second, flows of capital to emerging market economies in the form of purchases of securities

have increased greatly in size over the years and have substituted for other types of private capital. Third, when a crisis occurs new finance is unlikely to be forthcoming from those who undertook the original lending. These changes mean that financing available from official sources is less likely to be sufficient to enable a sovereign debtor experiencing a crisis to meet fully its external financing obligations. In any event, the Working Party stressed that provision of official funds to limit private losses raises serious moral hazard risks and could interfere with market discipline.

4. In considering means to deal with future sovereign liquidity crises, the Working Party was of the view that no single pre-set procedure can be suitable in all cases. However, it identified a broad set of desirable principles and features that provide a framework for the development of procedures for handling sovereign liquidity crises in a flexible, case-by-case approach in light of the conditions prevailing at the time, the nature and the intensity of the crises, and the circumstances of the debtor. Any such procedure should have the following features.
• It should foster sound economic policies by all debtors.
• It should minimise moral hazard for both creditors and debtors.
• It should rely on market forces and not interfere with the efficient operation of secondary markets in relevant debt instruments.
• It should limit contagion from one debtor's problems to other countries.
• It should support credible and sustainable actions and, to this end, not impose excessive social, political, or economic costs on the debtor.
• It should seek to ensure that burdens associated with the provision of exceptional financing are allocated fairly within and across different classes of creditors.
• It should strengthen the ability of governments to resist pressures to assume responsibility for the external liabilities of their private sectors.
• It should be suitable for quick and flexible use in a variety of different cases.
• It should be cooperative and non-confrontational, and promote the adoption by debtors and creditors of arrangements to facilitate resolution of liquidity crises should they occur.
• It should build on existing contractual or other arrangements that facilitate the resolution of crises.
• It should make use of existing practices and institutions.

5. The Working Party concluded that the establishment of a formal international bankruptcy procedure would not be feasible or appropriate under present circumstances or in the foreseeable future. Sovereign debtors have not in the past had a strong need for legal protection against their creditors, nor could they be obligated to submit to the jurisdiction of a bankruptcy forum. However, the Working Party noted that interested private parties might wish to continue to study the merits of bankruptcy or other formal procedures. At the same time, the Working Party concluded that it is not possible or desirable to preclude

official involvement altogether in the event of a serious crisis. The official community's interest in containing systemic risk and its role as a lender to sovereign borrowers mean that it is has a stake, and therefore a role to play, in fostering cooperative efforts by debtors and creditors to contend with unexpected payments problems.

6. In considering specific ways to facilitate resolution of sovereign liquidity crises, the Working Party took the view that current practices are an appropriate starting point. Current practices were developed over the course of the past few decades to contend with real world problems in a pragmatic and flexible manner. They are voluntary and make use of market information and market forces. The practices recognise the distinct perspectives of the three main actors involved in a crisis—the official community, private creditors, and the sovereign debtor—as well as their common interest in the orderly resolution of the crisis. They involve national authorities and multilateral institutions but place principal responsibility on the individual debtor and its creditors. The practices are based on the implementation of an IMF-supported sustainable adjustment programme as a major precondition for the cooperative resolution of a crisis.

7. The Working Party recognised that structural weaknesses in the banking systems of debtor countries could seriously aggravate liquidity crises and might pose difficulties for financial systems in lender countries. The Working Party concluded that further work should be undertaken in appropriate international forums to promote the strengthening of financial systems in emerging market economies and thus help to reduce such risks.

8. The Working Party took the view that certain contractual or statutory provisions governing debt contracts can facilitate the resolution of a crisis by fostering dialogue and consultation between the sovereign debtor and its creditors and among creditors, and by reducing the incentive for, or ability of, a small number of dissident creditors to disrupt, delay or prevent arrangements to support a credible adjustment programme that is acceptable to the vast majority of concerned parties. Among such provisions are those that (a) provide for the collective representation of debt holders in the event of crisis, (b) allow for qualified majority voting to alter the terms and conditions of debt contracts, and (c) require the sharing among creditors of assets received from the debtor. Such clauses have been employed in a limited set of debt contracts. The Working Party emphasised that evolution of contractual arrangements between sovereign borrowers and their creditors needs to be a market-led process if it is to be successful. Such efforts should receive official support as appropriate.

9. The Working Party strongly endorsed the fundamental principle that the terms and conditions of all debt contracts are to be met in full and on time. At the same time, it recognised that in certain exceptional cases the suspension of debt payments may be a necessary part of the crisis resolution process. Such

payment suspensions should be non-confrontational and implemented in a way that does not hamper the operation of secondary markets. The Working Party did not consider that it would be feasible to operate any formal mechanism for signalling the official community's approval of a suspension of payments by the debtor. Although the Working Party rejected any formal international approval of a suspension of debt payments, it concluded that it would be advisable for the IMF Executive Board to consider extending the scope of its current policy of lending, in exceptional circumstances, to a country that faces the prospect of continuing to accumulate arrears on some of its contractual debt-service obligations to private sector creditors, in cases where the country is undertaking a strong adjustment programme and making reasonable efforts to negotiate with its creditors. Such lending can both signal confidence in the debtor country's policies and longer-term prospects and indicate to unpaid creditors that their interests would best be served by quickly reaching an agreement with the debtor.

10.   The Working Party reached the overall conclusion that there is no need to change current procedures for official bilateral credits and long-term bank claims. However, there is a need for the principles and procedures for handling sovereign liquidity crises to take into account the new importance of debt in the form of securities and the growing likelihood that some such debt may have to be subject to renegotiation in the future. While the official community may be able to facilitate dialogue and assist in data collection, market participants should make the decisions regarding any innovations in contractual provisions. The official community's primary role in the resolution of sovereign liquidity crises should remain centred on the promotion of strong and effective adjustment by debtor countries in the context of IMF-supported programmes, which would need to take into account any recourse to temporary suspensions of payments.

PUBLICATIONS OF THE
INTERNATIONAL FINANCE SECTION

Notice to Contributors

The International Finance Section publishes papers in four series: ESSAYS IN INTERNATIONAL FINANCE, PRINCETON STUDIES IN INTERNATIONAL FINANCE, and SPECIAL PAPERS IN INTERNATIONAL ECONOMICS contain new work not published elsewhere. REPRINTS IN INTERNATIONAL FINANCE reproduce journal articles previously published by Princeton faculty members associated with the Section. The Section welcomes the submission of manuscripts for publication under the following guidelines:

ESSAYS are meant to disseminate new views about international financial matters and should be accessible to well-informed nonspecialists as well as to professional economists. Technical terms, tables, and charts should be used sparingly; mathematics should be avoided.

STUDIES are devoted to new research on international finance, with preference given to empirical work. They should be comparable in originality and technical proficiency to papers published in leading economic journals. They should be of medium length, longer than a journal article but shorter than a book.

SPECIAL PAPERS are surveys of research on particular topics and should be suitable for use in undergraduate courses. They may be concerned with international trade as well as international finance. They should also be of medium length.

Manuscripts should be submitted in triplicate, typed single sided and double spaced throughout on 8½ by 11 white bond paper. Publication can be expedited if manuscripts are computer keyboarded in WordPerfect 5.1 or a compatible program. Additional instructions and a style guide are available from the Section.

How to Obtain Publications

The Section's publications are distributed free of charge to college, university, and public libraries and to nongovernmental, nonprofit research institutions. Eligible institutions may ask to be placed on the Section's permanent mailing list.

Individuals and institutions not qualifying for free distribution may receive all publications for the calendar year for a subscription fee of $40.00. Late subscribers will receive all back issues for the year during which they subscribe. Subscribers should notify the Section promptly of any change in address, giving the old address as well as the new.

Publications may be ordered individually, with payment made in advance. ESSAYS and REPRINTS cost $8.00 each; STUDIES and SPECIAL PAPERS cost $11.00. An additional $1.50 should be sent for postage and handling within the United States, Canada, and Mexico; $1.75 should be added for surface delivery outside the region.

All payments must be made in U.S. dollars. Subscription fees and charges for single issues will be waived for organizations and individuals in countries where foreign-exchange regulations prohibit dollar payments.

Please address all correspondence, submissions, and orders to:

International Finance Section
Department of Economics, Fisher Hall
Princeton University
Princeton, New Jersey 08544-1021

List of Recent Publications

A complete list of publications may be obtained from the International Finance Section.

ESSAYS IN INTERNATIONAL FINANCE

166. John Spraos, *IMF Conditionality: Ineffectual, Inefficient, Mistargeted.* (December 1986)
167. Rainer Stefano Masera, *An Increasing Role for the ECU: A Character in Search of a Script.* (June 1987)
168. Paul Mosley, *Conditionality as Bargaining Process: Structural-Adjustment Lending, 1980-86.* (October 1987)
169. Paul A. Volcker, Ralph C. Bryant, Leonhard Gleske, Gottfried Haberler, Alexandre Lamfalussy, Shijuro Ogata, Jesús Silva-Herzog, Ross M. Starr, James Tobin, and Robert Triffin, *International Monetary Cooperation: Essays in Honor of Henry C. Wallich.* (December 1987)
170. Shafiqul Islam, *The Dollar and the Policy-Performance-Confidence Mix.* (July 1988)
171. James M. Boughton, *The Monetary Approach to Exchange Rates: What Now Remains?* (October 1988)
172. Jack M. Guttentag and Richard M. Herring, *Accounting for Losses On Sovereign Debt: Implications for New Lending.* (May 1989)
173. Benjamin J. Cohen, *Developing-Country Debt: A Middle Way.* (May 1989)
174. Jeffrey D. Sachs, *New Approaches to the Latin American Debt Crisis.* (July 1989)
175. C. David Finch, *The IMF: The Record and the Prospect.* (September 1989)
176. Graham Bird, *Loan-Loss Provisions and Third-World Debt.* (November 1989)
177. Ronald Findlay, *The "Triangular Trade" and the Atlantic Economy of the Eighteenth Century: A Simple General-Equilibrium Model.* (March 1990)
178. Alberto Giovannini, *The Transition to European Monetary Union.* (November 1990)
179. Michael L. Mussa, *Exchange Rates in Theory and in Reality.* (December 1990)
180. Warren L. Coats, Jr., Reinhard W. Furstenberg, and Peter Isard, *The SDR System and the Issue of Resource Transfers.* (December 1990)
181. George S. Tavlas, *On the International Use of Currencies: The Case of the Deutsche Mark.* (March 1991)
182. Tommaso Padoa-Schioppa, ed., with Michael Emerson, Kumiharu Shigehara, and Richard Portes, *Europe After 1992: Three Essays.* (May 1991)
183. Michael Bruno, *High Inflation and the Nominal Anchors of an Open Economy.* (June 1991)
184. Jacques J. Polak, *The Changing Nature of IMF Conditionality.* (September 1991)
185. Ethan B. Kapstein, *Supervising International Banks: Origins and Implications of the Basle Accord.* (December 1991)
186. Alessandro Giustiniani, Francesco Papadia, and Daniela Porciani, *Growth and Catch-Up in Central and Eastern Europe: Macroeconomic Effects on Western Countries.* (April 1992)
187. Michele Fratianni, Jürgen von Hagen, and Christopher Waller, *The Maastricht Way to EMU.* (June 1992)

188. Pierre-Richard Agénor, *Parallel Currency Markets in Developing Countries: Theory, Evidence, and Policy Implications.* (November 1992)

189. Beatriz Armendariz de Aghion and John Williamson, *The G-7's Joint-and-Several Blunder.* (April 1993)

190. Paul Krugman, *What Do We Need to Know About the International Monetary System?* (July 1993)

191. Peter M. Garber and Michael G. Spencer, *The Dissolution of the Austro-Hungarian Empire: Lessons for Currency Reform.* (February 1994)

192. Raymond F. Mikesell, *The Bretton Woods Debates: A Memoir.* (March 1994)

193. Graham Bird, *Economic Assistance to Low-Income Countries: Should the Link be Resurrected?* (July 1994)

194. Lorenzo Bini-Smaghi, Tommaso Padoa-Schioppa, and Francesco Papadia, *The Transition to EMU in the Maastricht Treaty.* (November 1994)

195. Ariel Buira, *Reflections on the International Monetary System.* (January 1995)

196. Shinji Takagi, *From Recipient to Donor: Japan's Official Aid Flows, 1945 to 1990 and Beyond.* (March 1995)

197. Patrick Conway, *Currency Proliferation: The Monetary Legacy of the Soviet Union.* (June 1995)

198. Barry Eichengreen, *A More Perfect Union? The Logic of Economic Integration.* (June 1996)

199. Peter B. Kenen, ed., with John Arrowsmith, Paul De Grauwe, Charles A. E. Goodhart, Daniel Gros, Luigi Spaventa, and Niels Thygesen, *Making EMU Happen—Problems and Proposals: A Symposium.* (August 1996)

200. Peter B. Kenen, ed., with Lawrence H. Summers, William R. Cline, Barry Eichengreen, Richard Portes, Arminio Fraga, and Morris Goldstein, *From Halifax to Lyons: What Has Been Done about Crisis Management?.* (October 1996)

PRINCETON STUDIES IN INTERNATIONAL FINANCE

58. John T. Cuddington, *Capital Flight: Estimates, Issues, and Explanations.* (December 1986)

59. Vincent P. Crawford, *International Lending, Long-Term Credit Relationships, and Dynamic Contract Theory.* (March 1987)

60. Thorvaldur Gylfason, *Credit Policy and Economic Activity in Developing Countries with IMF Stabilization Programs.* (August 1987)

61. Stephen A. Schuker, *American "Reparations" to Germany, 1919-33: Implications for the Third-World Debt Crisis.* (July 1988)

62. Steven B. Kamin, *Devaluation, External Balance, and Macroeconomic Performance: A Look at the Numbers.* (August 1988)

63. Jacob A. Frenkel and Assaf Razin, *Spending, Taxes, and Deficits: International-Intertemporal Approach.* (December 1988)

64. Jeffrey A. Frankel, *Obstacles to International Macroeconomic Policy Coordination.* (December 1988)

65. Peter Hooper and Catherine L. Mann, *The Emergence and Persistence of the U.S. External Imbalance, 1980-87.* (October 1989)

66. Helmut Reisen, *Public Debt, External Competitiveness, and Fiscal Discipline in Developing Countries.* (November 1989)

67. Victor Argy, Warwick McKibbin, and Eric Siegloff, *Exchange-Rate Regimes for a Small Economy in a Multi-Country World.* (December 1989)
68. Mark Gersovitz and Christina H. Paxson, *The Economies of Africa and the Prices of Their Exports.* (October 1990)
69. Felipe Larraín and Andrés Velasco, *Can Swaps Solve the Debt Crisis? Lessons from the Chilean Experience.* (November 1990)
70. Kaushik Basu, *The International Debt Problem, Credit Rationing and Loan Pushing: Theory and Experience.* (October 1991)
71. Daniel Gros and Alfred Steinherr, *Economic Reform in the Soviet Union: Pas de Deux between Disintegration and Macroeconomic Destabilization.* (November 1991)
72. George M. von Furstenberg and Joseph P. Daniels, *Economic Summit Declarations, 1975-1989: Examining the Written Record of International Cooperation.* (February 1992)
73. Ishac Diwan and Dani Rodrik, *External Debt, Adjustment, and Burden Sharing: A Unified Framework.* (November 1992)
74. Barry Eichengreen, *Should the Maastricht Treaty Be Saved?* (December 1992)
75. Adam Klug, *The German Buybacks, 1932-1939: A Cure for Overhang?* (November 1993)
76. Tamim Bayoumi and Barry Eichengreen, *One Money or Many? Analyzing the Prospects for Monetary Unification in Various Parts of the World.* (September 1994)
77. Edward E. Leamer, *The Heckscher-Ohlin Model in Theory and Practice.* (February 1995)
78. Thorvaldur Gylfason, *The Macroeconomics of European Agriculture.* (May 1995)
79. Angus S. Deaton and Ronald I. Miller, *International Commodity Prices, Macroeconomic Performance, and Politics in Sub-Saharan Africa.* (December 1995)
80. Chander Kant, *Foreign Direct Investment and Capital Flight.* (April 1996)

SPECIAL PAPERS IN INTERNATIONAL ECONOMICS

16. Elhanan Helpman, *Monopolistic Competition in Trade Theory.* (June 1990)
17. Richard Pomfret, *International Trade Policy with Imperfect Competition.* (August 1992)
18. Hali J. Edison, *The Effectiveness of Central-Bank Intervention: A Survey of the Literature After 1982.* (July 1993)
19. Sylvester W.C. Eijffinger and Jakob de Haan, *The Political Economy of Central-Bank Independence.* (May 1996)

REPRINTS IN INTERNATIONAL FINANCE

27. Peter B. Kenen, *Transitional Arrangements for Trade and Payments Among the CMEA Countries*; reprinted from *International Monetary Fund Staff Papers* 38 (2), 1991. (July 1991)
28. Peter B. Kenen, *Ways to Reform Exchange-Rate Arrangements*; reprinted from *Bretton Woods: Looking to the Future*, 1994. (November 1994)